Cottenham in Focus
A Pictorial History

The Cottenham Village Society

Published by
THE COTTENHAM VILLAGE SOCIETY
Information and Education Group
Cottenham, Cambridgeshire, UK

First published in 2002
Copyright © The Cottenham Village Society

All rights reserved. No part of this publication may be reproduced, stored in a retrieval system, or transmitted, in any form or by any means, electronic, mechanical, photocopying, recording or otherwise, without the prior permission, in writing, of the publisher.

ISBN 0-9543016-0-9

Design and production by
The Ellis Partners, Cambridge, UK

Printed in the UK by
Antony Rowe, Chippenham, Wiltshire

Acknowledgements

Liz Milway has compiled this publication in cooperation with Francis Garrett and Mervyn and Cynthia Haird. Other committee members of the Cottenham Village Society have given additional information and assistance.

Thanks are also due to Vara Hedge, Elizabeth and Ken Hewitt, Krys Kelly, T.F. Morris and Peter Sanderson.

The 'Committee' would also like to thank Eddie Murphy for the use of his map, and the many people who have over the years generously supplied Francis with information and Mervyn with photographs.

Sources

BULL, Arthur	Unpublished diaries, and typescript copies of his Parish Magazine entries, August 1893 to October 1901
FRIARS, Rev'd Ian	*A Short History of Cottenham and the Parish Church of All Saints*, 1996
GARRETT, Francis	*Cottenham: A Glimpse into the Past,* 1977 *A History of Cottenham's Inns and Hostelries*, 1989 *Cottenham, Cambridgeshire: The War Memorial*, 1993
GAUTREY, Horace	Unpublished diaries
MORTIMER, Richard	*Village Development and Ceramic Sequence: The Middle to Late Saxon village at Lordship Lane, Cottenham, Cambridgeshire* Proceedings of the Cambridge Antiquarian Society LXXXIX
PEACOCK, Olwyn	*Cottenham's Troubled Waters*, 1978 *Cottenham Commons & Cheeses*, 1984 *Cottenham's Orchards & Gardens: Domesday to 1990*, 1990 *Cottenham in Chaos: Life at the Time of the Enclosure*, 1996
RAVENSDALE, J.R.	*Liable to Floods: Village Landscape on the Edge of the Fens A.D.450-1850*, 1974
SEAR, Lawrence	*How Cottenham's Cheese Men Lost their Bread and Butter*, undated typescript
TAYLOR, Alison	*Archaeology of Cambridgeshire, Volume 2: South East Cambridgeshire and the Fen Edge*, 1998
Cottenham Village College Local History Group	*Charity School to Village College,* 1968

Previous Publications by the Village Society

1 *Cottenham: A Glimpse into the Past* (1977)

2 *Cottenham's Troubled Waters* (1978)

3 *Cottenham Ablaze* (1984)

4 *Cottenham Commons and Cheeses* (1984)

5 *Cottenham, Cambridgeshire, Monumental Inscriptions: The Parish Church of All Saints* (1988)

6 *A History of Cottenham's Inns and Hostelries* (1989)

7 *Cottenham's Orchards and Gardens: Domesday to 1990* (1990)

8 *Cottenham, Cambridgeshire, Monumental Inscriptions: The Dissenters' Cemetery* (1991/92)

9 *Cottenham, Cambridgeshire: The War Memorial* (1993)

10 *Cottenham in Chaos: Life at the Time of the Enclosure* (1996)

11 *Freeman Taylor 1814 –1860* (2001)

Dedication

To Francis Garrett and Mervyn Haird, for preserving and nurturing the social history of our village and without whom this book would not have been possible.

Francis Garrett has long been known in the village for his 'double act' with Mervyn Haird. Their slide show and local history presentation has entertained and informed the village since 1962.

Francis has spent most of his long lifetime collecting historical materials and gathering stories from local people. He was born in March 1920, and for a time, as the youngest person in the village, he lived in the same house as the oldest person in the village, his great-grandmother Mrs Ann Garrett, who died in 1922 in her hundredth year. He attended Margett Street School and then Cambridgeshire Technical College. He worked for Pye Radio in Cambridge before joining the Cambridgeshire Territorials in May 1939, when the threat of war hung over the world. He was captured during the Fall of Singapore on 15th February 1942 and transported into Thailand, where he spent the rest of the war in a series of prison camps, ending with a period in Changi. On his return, he worked in his late father's orchards until 1954, when he returned to work in the accounts section at Pye Radio. He married Nora in April 1948 and has two sons.

Francis says he has always been interested in stories about Cottenham, having grown up in a household surrounded by many older members of his family. His family kept the Jolly Millers public house, and he remembers learning his alphabet in the bar, with his Great Aunt Lizzie Smith. When he returned from the war, most of these older family members were dead, so he had to cast his net wider for stories of the village and its people. Francis has been a committee member of the Cottenham Village Society since its formation in 1970.

Mervyn Haird, who was born in Cottenham, was educated at Margett Street School and the County High School for Boys in Cambridge. From the age of 16, he spent forty-three years working with Pye Radio (later known as Phillips) as an electronic engineer until he retired in December 1980.

With his family tree dating back to 1630, and following three generations of the Haird family who were schoolmasters and Parish Clerks, Mervyn inherited a very keen and valuable interest in local affairs and the history of Cottenham. He served on the Parish Council for fifteen years, was a Trustee of Cottenham United Charities for twenty years, a founder member of the Village Society and is still a Trustee of the Cottenham British School Trust. He has been Treasurer of Cottenham Dissenters' Cemetery since 1976.

He became interested in photography in 1946 and in 1962 he acquired a large quantity of negatives from the local photographer Fred Smith. This started his collection of Cottenham slides. With the help of local people who lent him photos to copy, he has amassed a collection that now stands at 3,400 slides, which he takes much pleasure in showing both locally and countywide. He also provides photographs and historic material for local displays and exhibitions.

Contents

	A Brief Introduction to Cottenham	8
	Village Map	10
Chapter 1	The High Street	11
	The Green	11
	Round the Green to Lack's Close	14
	Charles Lack & Sons	25
	Denmark Road to Lambs Lane	29
	Around the Village Sign	48
	Salvation Army Hall to the Three Horseshoes	56
	Whitehead's Bicycle Factory	67
	The Royal British Legion to the Church	71
	Twentypence Road	93
Chapter 2	Exploring the Side Streets	96
	Ivatt Street to Tenison Manor	96
	The Lanes	100
	Lambs Lane to Histon Road	120
Chapter 3	Rural Industries	132
Chapter 4	Pastimes	149

A Brief Introduction to Cottenham

People have been visiting the land on which our village stands since prehistoric times, and scattered discoveries of Mesolithic and Neolithic tools have been made around Cottenham. There was a late Bronze Age settlement at Lingwood Farm, to the north of the village. One of the earliest wheels found in Britain was preserved in the damp fen soil here, close to the River Ouse.

There were at least seven small centres of Roman occupation within Cottenham, but the nearest large Roman settlement was at Bullocks Haste by the side of Car Dyke, about a mile to the north of the village. The remains can be spotted, as uneven ground, from the footpath along the Cottenham Lode, between the road to Smithy Fen and the river. Roman artefacts found in the area include a bust of Emperor Commodus from Bullocks Haste and a hoard of over 5,000 coins dating from the late third century, found in a pot in a Roman field ditch in 1986.

The origin of the name Cottenham appears to be Saxon, arising from the early English 'Cotan' for dwelling and 'ham' for settlement. Recent archaeological excavations have found what seems to be the core of this Saxon settlement, in the centre of today's village.

Cottenham is known to have been one of the largest villages in Cambridgeshire from the eleventh century. There were six medieval manors with landholdings in the village - Crowland, Lyles, Sames, Rectory, Burdeleys (which later became Harlestons) and Pelhams. The largest manor, Crowland, was part of the Crowland Abbey estate in Lincolnshire. It was recorded in the twelfth century that Crowland Manor, along with the neighbouring manor of Oakington, was given to the Abbey by Turketel, some time before he became Abbot of Crowland in AD971. Turketel was a grandson of Alfred the Great and the Chancellor of the Kingdom under his cousin, King Athelstan. Most of Turketel's estates had been given to him by his uncle King Edward - the eldest son of Alfred - but it is not certain whether Cottenham was included in this gift.

Ingulph's *History of the Abbey of Croyland* records that in *c*1010, 'The Danes, making incursions throughout the provinces, stripping the inhabitants of all that was movable, and burning all that could not be carried away, pillaged [Dry] Drayton, Cottenham, and Oakington manors belonging to Croyland, and ravaged them, together with the whole county of Cambridge, with flames'.

The manors of Oakington and Cottenham were rebuilt between 1017 and 1032 and when the Domesday Book was compiled in 1086, Cottenham had a population of about 350 inhabitants.

According to tradition, Cottenham played a part in the establishment of the University of Cambridge. When in 1109 the Abbey at Crowland was destroyed in a fire, four learned monks - Gilbert, Odo, Terric and William - were billeted at the Cottenham Manor. They hired a barn in Cambridge, to lecture daily on theology and logic, raising funds for the rebuilding of the Abbey. They were able to send 100 marks a year to the Abbey at Crowland.

The full length of the High Street is thought to have been built upon by the late thirteenth century. Cottenham's High Street is known to be one of the longest in the country, measuring one and a quarter miles from the Green to the church.

The Parish Church of All Saints was built in the Perpendicular style of architecture used during the fifteenth century. The distinctive tower was built in 1617-19, replacing a steeple destroyed by a gale. In the later part of the seventeenth century Cottenham was part of the nonconformist movement; the village gained several chapels, and a cemetery for dissenters was opened in 1845.

Cottenham was recorded in 1596 as one of only twenty-two Cambridgeshire parishes to have a schoolmaster, although the school was subsequently destroyed when the church steeple fell in 1617.

Throughout the centuries the village of Cottenham has had links with some famous families. There are records of the Pepys family in the village since 1273, but in the late sixteenth century John of Cottenham moved to Impington where he died in 1589. His great-grandson was Samuel Pepys, the famous diarist. The present Earl of Cottenham is another descendant of the Pepys family.

The name Coolidge, which in common with most names of the time was spelt in various ways, appears in the Parish Registers from 1572 until the late seventeenth century. The family from whom the American president Calvin Coolidge was descended emigrated from Cottenham in 1630.

Two thirds of Cottenham was destroyed by fire in 1676, and further fires between 1847 and 1855 led to the uniformity of building style that gave rise to the term 'Cottenham Villa'. Most of the older houses along the High Street were farmhouses, and each had farmyards and barns. Cottenham was primarily a farming village until the mid-twentieth century. Before the Parliamentary Enclosure of 1842 changed the shape of landholdings, Cottenham farmers practised dairying and mixed agriculture. The emphasis changed to market gardening in the late nineteenth century, though it has returned to agriculture since the 1960s.

Victory Way and Orchard Close were built shortly after the Second World War, with most houses on each estate built around a central green. Coolidge Gardens was constructed in the early 1960s. The large green area at the entrance to the estate was the site of the Garibaldi Pond. The village gained several new streets in the late 1960s when the houses on Ellis Close, Lyles Road, Pelham Way, Dunstal Field and later, Wilkin Walk, were built.

In 1977 Cottenham marked the Silver Jubilee of Queen Elizabeth II with a week of celebrations. All children under twelve years of age were given a mug to celebrate the occasion. There were so many events organised by committee groups that there was a 'Jubilee Box Office'. Francis Garrett wrote a small booklet for the Cottenham Village Society entitled *Cottenham: A Glimpse into the Past*. It is still in demand, twenty-five years later, and was the beginning of a series of publications by the Society.

Since 1977, Cottenham has expanded enormously. In the past twelve years, Courtyard Way, Curringtons Close, The Rowells, Manse Drive and Lee Close have been built. Four hundred new homes were added to the village in the late 1990s with the construction of two new large housing estates - Tenison Manor and Brenda Gautrey Way. Cottenham's population is now in excess of 5,000.

Cottenham continues to be an active village, with many sports, social and educational groups helping to maintain a sense of community. The Parish Council celebrated its centenary in June 1994 with a gala on the Green that included a visit from the Band of the Grenadier Guards and a flypast by a Hercules bomber from RAF Mildenhall. The fiftieth anniversaries of V.E. and V.J. Days in 1995 were commemorated with a thanksgiving at the War Memorial attended by the Band of the Royal Marines School of Music, another flypast by 'Percy' from RAF Mildenhall, and a gala on the Green. Echoing the Silver Jubilee, all children under the age of twelve were given souvenir mugs to celebrate the Millennium.

This book of local photographs and stories has been prepared for Queen Elizabeth II's Golden Jubilee celebrations, by members of Cottenham Village Society, as a further contribution to the story of our village.

We now take you on a photographic journey through the history of our village, travelling along the High Street, from the Green to All Saints Church, and then northwards to the river on Twentypence Road. On the return journey, we explore the streets to the north west, the 'Lanes' to the south east and the roads to the south of the High Street.

A Map of Cottenham

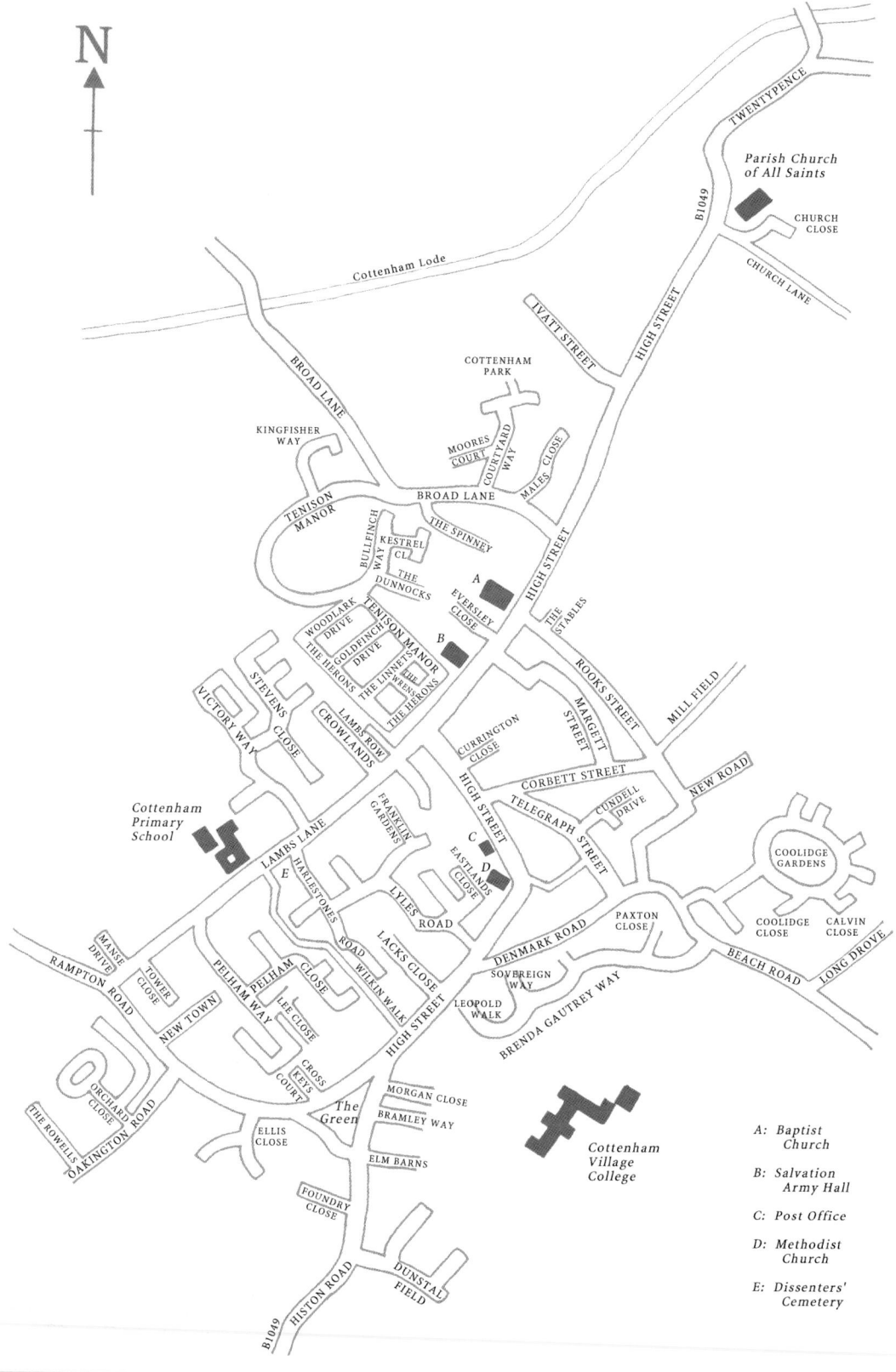

THE HIGH STREET

The High Street from the Green to the intersection with Denmark Road was formerly known as Green End.

The Green

The Green in 1907
Robert Ivatt planted the trees shown here in 1885. The cows feeding on the Green belonged to William Coxall, who lived at 333 High Street; his grandson Osbourne 'Orb' Collins and another herdsman are pictured tending the cows.

The pond on the Green

The pond, which was at the War Memorial end of the Green, was at one time known as the Weir. The County Council planted the trees at this end of the Green. By 1927 the pond was in a sad state, having last been cleaned out forty-two years earlier at a cost of £15. In 1925 it had been resolved that £20 should be spent to clean out the pond, but in the intervening two years only £1 of that allocated money had been spent. The Parish Council then requested that the remaining £19 be spent to use the pond as a dumping ground, until it was filled in. The sludge cart had long been used to clear mud from the village streets and tip it into the pond, so it was an unhealthy mud hole. Once the pond was filled in, the Green would be a much healthier place for children to play.

The filling in of the pond was the occasion for the first collection of non-burnable rubbish in the village. Until then, people mostly dug pits in their back yards to bury tins, bottles, etc.

The roadway across the Green

The Green used to have a roadway through its centre, from the current pillar-box on one side to the lay-by. The pump was by this roadway and about thirty feet from the edge of the pond. Water was drawn from the pump for Church End during the typhoid epidemics from 1885 until 1903, because some water sources at Church End were found to be contaminated. By April 1928 the pond had been filled in, and the surveyor thought the pump should be moved and the roadway removed. This was carried out in 1932. The Village Society brought the pump that is now on the Green from Church End in 1985.

Snow on the Green in the severe winter of 1947

A clockwise walk around the Green starting from the Village College.

333 High Street – The Limes, photographed in 2002
The Limes is a 17th century timber framed house with an early 19th century brick-built dairy on the side and a lattice window for the cheese room above.

337 High Street
This is a late 17th century house, home of the Collins family until 1972. There was a cheese press in the dairy; the pressed cheeses were passed through a hole in the dairy ceiling to the cheese room above. The cheeses were hung in this room for twelve months. The roof was thatched directly onto the rafters, and there was no ceiling. Cottenham was famous for its cheese until production ended during the cattle plague in 1865. Note the post box on the wall.

343 High Street – The Elms, photographed in 2002

The house was built in 1851 for £600. The Ivatt family claimed to have lived on this site for four hundred years. In that time, three of the Ivatt family were named William and seven were named Thomas. The seventh Thomas died in 1926, leaving two daughters. The last member of this Cottenham family, Ethel Annie, died in 1961.

The seventh Thomas Ivatt

A court case took place in 1893 following one of the last known Cottenham examples of tin-kettling. Tin-kettling was an old custom, in which members of the community publicly shamed errant husbands. From the evidence given in court on 23rd December, a crowd of young men, including John Rayment, William Collins, William Badcock, Arthur Cox and Frank Pettit assembled outside Mr Ivatt's house on 18th December 1893. They created a noise by beating old kettles and pails, hooting and yelling and using threatening language towards Thomas Ivatt. Each of the men was fined one shilling and costs.

In the 1970s, the artist John Hutton lived in the house, and worked on engraved glass panels for Coventry Cathedral in his studio. He engraved his own designs of flying and standing angels and saints. The glass panels make up the great wall at the west end of the cathedral.

358 High Street

Hart's Foundry started at 13 Histon Road in Hobson's House, before moving to the Green in the 1880s. John Hart had come from Barley in Hertfordshire in 1862.

Harts did the castings for Charles Lack, the local engineering firm, in a tall brick barn at the rear of the property. When the foundry was in operation, you could see the flames roaring at least four feet above the top of the chimney. The foundry closed in 1946.

Clockwise from the left are Willie Harris, Albert Pauley, Harry Pauley, William Hart, John Hart junior and Mr Keble.

A canning machine made for Chivers of Histon
The machine was used to apply rubber solution or cornflour paste to cans used for fruit.

344-346 High Street

Roger Harleston had his manor sacked during the Peasants' Revolt, which occurred in 1381. Several pieces of repressive legislation, culminating in the Poll Tax of 1380, led to the uprising. Roger Harleston's properties at Cottenham, Haslingfield, Milton and Stapleford were violently attacked because he was both a Poll Tax Commissioner and an envied successful businessman.

The manor of Harleston was sold to Christ's College, Cambridge, in the 16th century and the estate remained intact until about fifty years ago. Four generations of the Hall family leased the manor from 1801. The initials on the chimney, T & AH, refer to Thomas and Anne Hall, who lived in this house after Christ's College built it in 1868. The Lewin family took over the house in 1893, and this side view of the house was photographed after a chimney was struck by lightning in 1909. The house, with some of the land, was sold to Samuel Fletcher for £2,700 in the 1970s.

The Cross Keys public house

Gardiner's Directory commented about the village in 1851, 'The men of this place were formerly so noted for drinking that they were called the Cottenham Gulpers'. There were thirty-four public houses and beer houses in Cottenham in 1869, when the population was just 2,414.

In 1917, Ernest Smith, the publican of the Cross Keys, was summonsed for serving soldiers from the Voluntary Aid Detachment (V.A.D.) hospital in the village during prohibited hours, and lost his licence.

328 High Street

The house currently occupying this site was built in 1893 and sold at auction in 1952 for £1,200 to its tenant Fred Smith. An earlier house on this site was known as 'Burgoins at the Weir' and was one of three Cottenham houses bought by Hobson's Charity in 1632 to earn rental income for the Spinning House in Cambridge, which was both a workhouse and a house of correction for women.

326 High Street

Mr and Mrs Thoday made a fruit drink called 'Penny Monster', which they sold from their shop on the site. On 15th June 1931, a fire started in their roof and the local fire engine, which had been stored in the Engine House for years, was called. There was considerable effort expended cutting the thick grass obstructing the doors, but the engine could not be got out. The equipment for the hydrants was stored at David Ingles' workshop, almost opposite the Jolly Millers public house, way down the High Street. Sidney Pratt and 'Archer' Porter loaded up the hoses and brought them down the High Street in a wheelbarrow. Despite the urgency of the situation, 'Archer' Porter stopped to light his pipe three or four times on the way. The Chivers fire engine, called from Histon, and the Cambridge fire engine eventually arrived, but the Cottenham one never did!

324 High Street

This early 18th century red brick house was the only property in Cottenham copyhold (the nearest equivalent to this archaic form of tenure is leasehold) of the manor of St Etheldreda in Histon. Before the Enclosure most other village properties were copyhold to one of the manors in Cottenham.

In the early 19th century Henry Fullston, the wheelwright, lived in this house. He stacked his wood along the roadside.

In the late 1920s Mary Franklin lived here. She was the first woman in the village brave enough to wear shorts and trousers. She used to visit the school to collect money for a dogs' home. In November 1929, she gave prizes to two pupils, Christine Hopkins and Joan Cole, for an essay about dogs.

An example of Cottenham's famous iron railings

316 High Street

The house known locally as 'Raspberry Castle' was built by Azariah Gautrey senior in 1885 and was owned by the family until Cecil Gautrey died in 1991. It had a little shop in the right hand front corner. The family came from Soham in 1790. They were fruit-growers, and it is said that three or four good seasons of raspberries had enabled them to replace most of the old timber-framed building with a brick three-storey house.

Further on in the picture is the white house used by Betsy Woods as a Dame School in the 1860s, which was demolished in 1923.

The Village College site

This 15th century house was one of the buildings demolished in 1962 to build the Village College. It had survived the fires of 1827 and 1847, and was converted into two cottages in 1860. At the beginning of the 19th century, it was the home of Richard Bacchus, and was later owned by James Ivatt, William Peed and then Ephraim Gautrey. It shows the character of many houses along the High Street before the fires. To the right of these cottages was the home of James Ivatt, known as the wealthiest man in Cottenham when he died in 1870. He owned 600 acres of land, ten houses and £16,000 in cash. His total wealth was thought to be over £100,000. It was left to his only daughter Mrs Sumpter of Histon who, when she died in 1877, left most of it to her solicitor William Peed. In the early 1890s his son, Wilton Peed, installed the first bathroom in Cottenham. Ephraim Gautrey purchased the two buildings on their 18 acres of land, together with over 300 acres of land beside Rampton Road, in 1899 for £8,200. Mr Gautrey's daughter, Mrs Elizabeth Haird, sold just the houses together with their 18 acres in June 1956 for £7,000 for the Village College. Work on the college began in 1960, and classes began in September 1963. Her Majesty Queen Elizabeth, The Queen Mother, performed the Official Opening on 7th November 1963.

The pond at the front of the college was at the rear of the larger house, and is still known as 'Gautrey's Pond'.

300-302 High Street – The Homestead

The original house, which was sited on what is now the walled garden, burnt down in 1855. The new house was then built, along with the farmyard. The barn had doors at the front and back split into three levels. The lower part, about two feet high, was designed to slide out, above this came two large doors, and two smaller doors at the highest level. This arrangement allowed horse, and later, tractor drawn loads to pass through the barn directly into the rickyard behind it. Grain might also occasionally be in heaps up to six feet high in the barn, or spread over the floor to a depth of about two feet. The lower parts of the barn doors were there to contain the corn. Mr Morris replaced the roof of the barn in the early 1970s with the aim of growing orchids commercially. He fitted a watertight wooden floor at roof level, and above it a roof of Perspex. The external walkway was constructed to help with roof maintenance. Unfortunately, his stock of plants was lost when a frost coincided with the temporary halting of fuel oil sales during the fuel crisis.

296 High Street

Frank Cross, who lived at Hemsel House, was the only Cottenham man who went to the Gold Rush on the Klondyke in the late 1890s. He returned to the village, but it is uncertain how much gold he had found.

MRS MOORE GREEN END HAND LAUNDRY HIGH ST COTTENHAM

315 High Street

The widow of Herbert Moore kept the Green End Hand Laundry at Marland House between 1909 and 1916. The laundry was renowned for the special attention given to the washing of flannel clothing.

290 High Street - Charles Lack & Sons

Lack's House
The house was built about 1820 and was the first one in Cottenham built from brick and slate. Charles Lack came to Cottenham in 1872. Charles Lack and Sons were agricultural engineers and well sinkers. They became a limited company in 1912 and employed thirty-two people by 1932. The business was sold to Melford Engineering in 1966 and closed in 1972.

Outside Lack's Yard
Charlie Goodwin, a fruit haulier from Loughborough, chatting with a villager outside Lack's Yard. Mr Goodwin stayed in the village during the fruit season, carrying the produce to Oakington station in his car.

Lack's Yard in 1972

The men's working day was regulated by a hooter, driven by compressed air, that could be heard all over the village. Arthur 'Tipper' Smith was the timekeeper. Work started when the men clocked in at 6.30 a.m. The hooter first sounded at 8 a.m. and the men went home for breakfast until 8.30 a.m. It sounded again at 1 p.m. for lunch, when the men went home until 2 p.m. The working day ended with the hooter sounding at 5 p.m. Many people in the village used to set their clocks by it.

The hooter was also used as an air-raid warning siren for the village in the Second World War, until proper sirens were installed. It was first sounded for this purpose in the early days of the war when an unidentified aircraft flew over the East Anglian coast.

Lack's commercial dishwashing machine, c1905
This machine was designed for hotels and restaurants. It was claimed that well over two thousand pieces of crockery could be 'perfectly cleansed' in an hour. It was never used in Cottenham!

A jelly-cutting machine being made by Lacks for Chivers of Histon before the First World War
From the left are Jack Kilborn, unknown, Frank Peck, Hubert Diddell, Stanley Kimpton, Archie Bennerson, and the boy is Reginald Cross.

A Triple Deep Well Pump being made
In the photograph are Bert Lack, Stanley Kimpton, Ernest Bell and John Lee. It is known that the photograph was taken before the First World War, as sadly Bert Lack was killed during the war.

The Lathe-Shop
This photograph was also taken before the First World War. The man holding the wheel is Bert Lack. The man with a moustache is Hubert Diddell and the joker with the washer in his eye is Ernest Bell.

A report of the fire of 1676 entitled 'A sad relation of a dreadful fire at Cottenham' stated that the High Street from this point was known as Church Street. It had earlier still been known as Fenning Street.

The War Memorial

The War Memorial was unveiled in 1921 in honour of the fifty-nine local men killed in the First World War. In 1920, after considerable deliberation, the Parish Council had chosen to have a stone monument erected in front of the Chequers public house and an oak tablet placed in the church, rather than a memorial elsewhere (other places suggested were in front of the Constitutional Club, in the churchyard or on the Green), or an institute for ex-soldiers. Fred Bacchus of Histon was the architect and contractor and charged £544 6s 0d. Messrs John Hart & Son, the village iron-founders, were paid ten guineas for the ironwork. The entire cost was met by public subscription.

An aerial view of the War Memorial, the Chequers public house and the High Street before Lyles Road was constructed

The Chequers public house and Denmark Road in 1910

Ralph Carpenter recalls seeing, under the bed in the big bedroom of the Chequers, four patches on the floor which puzzled him until he read Horace Gautrey's diary entry for Tuesday, 1st March 1949. A chimney stack at the public house blew down in the early hours of that morning, it fell through the roof and onto a bedstead with such force that the legs of the bed were forced through the floorboards. The occupants of the house were unhurt.

On the left is William Sanderson's farm building, c1900

Next left is Carter's bakery shop, Bennett's, the harness makers, and the Bennett's thatched house. Across the road and behind the black fence was Westrope, the village printer. The low thatched building was the butcher's shop (replaced by a modern shop, but still the butcher). The thatched roof of Queenholme is just visible, and the Co-operative Store is in the background.

The Munsey family house on the left and part of this row of shops (converted for Ernest Munsey from what had once been William Sanderson's cart shed) were demolished to build Lyles Road. The shops in this row included a fish shop, Drayton Trading and the Ideal Library which was run by Mrs Ulrich.

266 High Street

The Bennett family were harness makers for more than four generations. In the photograph you can see Alfred Bennett, John Warren and some of their horse collars. In the background is Eastlands Garage.

Kneecaps for elephants

Bennett's harness makers supplied varied leather goods including the harness for a state coach and dressage saddles for an Australian equestrian team, but perhaps their strangest commission was when Edward Bennett made kneecaps for elephants. These were for the Cambridge University's attempt to retrace Hannibal's journey across the Alps.

260 High Street

Outside Eastlands Garage, which was established in 1908, is a motorcycle owned by Forrest Adamson. Fred Ward owned the motorcycle with the sidecar which was used to carry milk churns. In the photograph are Jack Diddell, E.G.Haird, Vic Haird, Tom Male, Walter Kimpton, Eddie Smith, John Hart and Fred Ward.

Frederick Vialls' cart

Frederick Vialls had an elegant carrier's cart at the beginning of the 20th century. If you booked your seat, he would come to pick you up and take you to Cambridge on Saturdays. Passengers would sit along each side and if there were a lot of children, he would place a plank across between the adults and the children would sit in the middle.

279 High Street - Queenholme

Originally built in the late 16th century, the house has a steeply pitched roof and was originally jetted on the first floor, before being under-built. Queenholme is possibly the oldest house still standing in Cottenham and has belonged to the same family since 1797. Richard Norman senior bought the house. His son Richard Norman junior, who had farmed Queenholme Farm in Willingham, lived in it after he retired. The house passed down the maternal line to the Burgess family.

The Wesleyan Chapel

The Methodist Church, originally known as the Wesleyan Chapel, was built in 1864 and the manse was built in 1866. Cottenham Methodism had an interesting beginning. Mr Thomas Ivatt senior, who was an Anglican, married a Baptist lady, Mary Ann Goode. Their first child, who died in the 1840s at the age of six, had not been baptised. The rector of the parish refused to bury the child and a Baptist minister had to read the service outside the churchyard. Mr Ivatt was incensed at this treatment and asked the Methodists from Cambridge to come to Cottenham to conduct services. Mr Ivatt lent them a barn until more suitable premises were found in Telegraph Street. There was already a small Primitive Methodist congregation in Cottenham.

The Wesleyan Choir in 1910

In the back row are Hubert Diddell, Leonard Wolfe, Evelyn Lack, Thomas Ivatt and Mr Carter.

In the front row are Olive Furbank, Dorothy Pierson, Nellie Hatley, unknown, unknown, Lizzie Thoday and Miss Ivatt.

Nurse Gooby's Mothers and Babies Group

Nurse Gooby, the Cottenham District Nurse, with her Mothers and Babies Group held at the Wesleyan Chapel. This photograph dates from 1917, the year she left.

From the left on the back row are Mrs R. Bennerson and Gwen, Mrs Ted Badcock and Arthur, Mrs Tom Peck and Elsie, unknown, unknown.

On the middle row are Mrs Jack Johnson and Reginald, Mrs John Lee and Norman, Mrs Pettit and Mollie, unknown, unknown, Mrs Arthur Barnes and Reginald.

On the front row are Mrs Jeffrey and Barbara, Nurse Gooby, Mrs Jack Tibbett and Enid, Mrs Robert Hostler and Gwendolyn.

The Co-operative Store c1920, with the manager, Charles Walker, Daisy Anderson and Alice Butler

Godfrey Morlin Goode, the eminent tea dealer, constructed the building in about 1780. In January 1854, when James Male had a grocery business in the building, he sent William Symonds to Waterbeach for a cartload of salt. On his return journey, William fell from the cart and was killed when the wheel passed over his head. It was thought he was 'tipsy'. The business transferred to the Co-operative Society in 1905.

257-259 High Street

The white house to the right of the top photograph, and in the centre right of the second photograph, was demolished half at a time. Jonathan Piggott who had owned the whole property left it to his two daughters, Mrs Bertha Munsey and Mrs Alfred Moore. The first half was pulled down when Mrs Alfred Moore built the Coronation Villa in 1902, with the second half remaining until much more recently.

225 High Street

Todd's Store was on the corner of Telegraph Street. Sweets were sold here in cones made from rolled up paper with a little twist at the bottom. There were witnesses still alive in 1963 who recalled that when one of the shopkeeper's daughters weighed out the sweets, she would be so reluctant to give more than the correct amount that she would pick one up, bite it in half, and throw the excess half back into the jar for the next customer.

220 High Street – Gothic House

Gothic House was built in the 1730s and was a red brick house similar to Oaslands House at 4 Broad Lane. It was bought by the Ivatt family in 1770 and greatly altered around 1860. The porch was erected, the ground floor lowered and the decorative chimneys were built at that time. It was sold in 1913 to Fred Chivers for £875 and then purchased by Philip Franklin in 1943.

Mr Ivatt's horseless carriage
Robert Ivatt, farmer, maltster and miller, owned the first motorised vehicle in the village. Mr Ivatt is shown driving with his daughter in about 1895. His engineer, George Barnes, is standing by.

219–221 High Street - The Limes, photographed in 2002
This house was the surgery and residence for two generations of Cottenham doctors. Dr Cox was succeeded by his son-in-law Dr Ellis in 1921. There is a door on the left side of the building opening to a passageway, which was the waiting area for the surgery.

Curringtons Close

This is the earliest known photograph of Cottenham. It was taken at Male's brewery prior to 1871; William Wright, seen on the far right, died before the 1871 census. The brewery buildings were demolished to build Curringtons Close.

215 High Street

The 1898 Cottenham Cricket team prepare to leave the White Horse public house for Stretham. From the left are Duke Ivatt, Ernest Chivers, Joe Ward, Thomas Haird, Solomon Piggott, Charles Todd, Herbert Simpkins, and Ebenezer Chivers. On the front seat are Herbert Male, Jack Pauley and Dr Cox.

213A High Street

The Post Office was located at various sites along the High Street over the years. From its beginnings at the Pepys School with Thomas Haird in 1843, it moved to Cottenham Supply Stores on the corner of Lambs Lane with Sarah Chambers in 1862. Henry Franklin, the chemist, took it over at 213A High Street from 1869 until it returned to Cottenham Supply Stores with W.C. Graves in 1883. In 1890, the Post Office returned to 213A High Street and the care of Arthur Holdgate, who was the post master and chemist for nearly forty years until he died in 1929. He had taken over the chemist shop from Henry Franklin in 1880. After Mr Holdgate's death, his daughter Brenda carried on the business until it closed in 1973. At this time, the Post Office moved across the road to its present site. Arthur Holdgate can be seen outside his shop with his assistant Arthur Young. Note the post box on the side.

Between 209 and 213 High Street

Percy Hankin is shown shoeing Harold Bicheno's horse at the blacksmith's shop owned by William Butler. The smithy survived the fires of 1850, and finally closed in 1974. William Butler used to manufacture a variety of agricultural implements, including horse harrows.

A stone grinder used by the blacksmith

204 High Street

In 1851 John Chambers opened Cottenham Supply Stores on the corner of Lambs Lane. The shop is shown in 1901, at which time William 'Billy' Graves had been the proprietor for nineteen years. Mr Graves also provided transport to and from Oakington Station; if he did not have any other vehicle available, he would send his hearse to pick people up!

Tom King, the rag-and-bone man, used to go around the village collecting scrap. He would then visit Mr Graves, who bought anything usable from him. Local people might then identify articles they had given to the rag-and-bone man on sale at Billy Graves' store.

Cottenham Supply Stores – shop window in 1901
The front of the store changed greatly over the years. It was used for several drapery businesses and then as a car showroom before becoming derelict. In the 1990s it was renovated and now houses several flats.

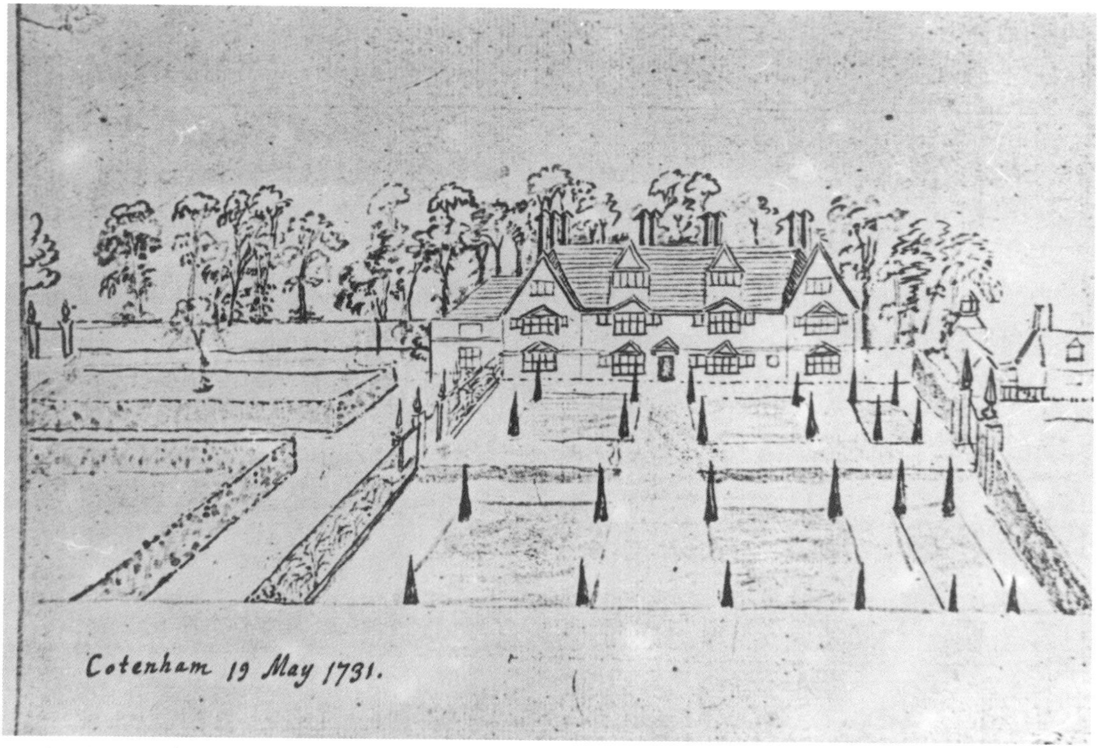

Cotenham 19 May 1731.

A sketch of Lordship House, drawn by the antiquarian William Stukely in 1731 during the ownership of Roger Gale

Lordship House

Thomas and Rose Saintey and the Bowers family stand outside Lordship House in the 1890s

Thomas Hobson purchased the manors of Crowland, Lyles and part of the manor of Sames in 1625. He was the celebrated Cambridge carrier. The expression 'Hobson's Choice' arose from his method of hiring out horses in strict rotation. His grandson, also named Thomas Hobson, lived in Lordship House, the mansion house of the manor of Lyles. The Lordship estate, with its mansion, yards, gardens and park, extended from what is now Crowlands roadway, along Lambs Lane and the High Street to the doctor's surgery.

In 1669, Thomas Hobson's widow Katherin married John Pepys, of the famous Impington family, said to be 'a match which allowed him to live in a house with a dozen fireplaces'. Katherin's granddaughter, Alice Rogers, bequeathed the Cottenham estates to Roger Gale when she died in 1728. The estates were sold in 1737 to Edward Snagg and then divided in 1770 when Thomas Bacchus took up residence in Lordship House. In 1801 the Lordship estate was sold in plots, with access from a new lane known as Lordship Lane. The house, yard, and all the land fronting Lambs Lane was bought by Ellis Munsey, a Cottenham builder. A keen Baptist, he sold the dovehouse, built of stud, plaster and thatch, to the Baptists of Waterbeach, where it was re-erected and became a chapel where C.H. Spurgeon, a famous preacher, spoke.

The Philo Union Reading Room was established in the parish in 1853. The word philo is an abbreviation of philology, the definition being the science of languages.

The Cottenham Club, until recently known as the Conservative Club

Fred Smith, a member of the Cottenham threshing machine family, went to Africa where he made a fortune from a diamond mine. When he returned in 1895 he gave the old people and children of the village a high tea. Wanting to make a more permanent contribution to the village he purchased Lordship House together with the neighbouring cottages, demolished the old Philo and commissioned the local company, Rayments, to build the Victoria Institute.

On completion, there were no further funds for the maintenance of the building. The Victoria Institute was acquired by Mr John Morlin Goode of Mitchell House and the name was changed to the Constitutional Club. Mr Goode died in 1930. His widow, Elizabeth Amelia, left the building to the Cottenham and Rampton Conservative Association when she died in 1932. The building became the Conservative Club.

Mr Kirby of Over opened the Electric Cinema in the Lordship Hall at the rear of the Constitutional Club on Tuesday 24th August 1920. Subsequently, Cecil Symonds, also from Over, ran the cinema on Thursday evenings during the early 1920s until the start of the Second World War. The film projector was in his Morris van parked at the rear of the building and the film was projected through a small hole in the wall onto a screen in the hall. Cecil also visited Willingham, Swavesey and Linton with his travelling cinema van.

Cecil Symonds was a radio engineer and a local 'ham' (amateur radio operator). During the Second World War, in collaboration with Mr Mustill, he built a radio set capable of establishing communications with occupied Burma.

The demolition of Lordship House
Ellis Munsey pulled down part of Lordship House and built several small cottages along Lambs Lane *c*1801. Several years later the remaining part of the house was divided into three tenements, but gradually fell into disrepair and was razed to the ground in 1937. The photograph shows Maurice Gautrey and Horace Ward helping with the demolition.

Adams Ale is the best brew!

This Temperance Gathering was photographed *c*1900 from the balcony of the Victoria Institute. Rather ironically, the Black Horse Brewery, now 205-207 High Street, can be seen in the background!

James Chivers bought the premises at 205-207 High Street in 1826. He built the brewhouse and was selling beer and spirits in the 1830s. Following his death, his sons Ebenezer and James ran the brewing business until they dissolved the partnership in October 1862. James' portion of stock in trade - 6 pockets of hops, 50 barrels, 15 kilderkins and 35 firkins - was auctioned. Ebenezer continued brewing until he sold the public house and brewery to P.R. Holben in 1892. John Bartingale remained as publican for 15 years, the licence being transferred to John Kent in 1894, and Herbert Ward in 1896. Brewing was still carried on under the management of Ebenezer's son, Fred Chivers, until 1897.

On Saturday 25 September 1897, by direction of P.R. Holben, 'the well known public house known as the 'Black Horse' with 4 quarter brewery' was sold by auction at the Lion Hotel, Cambridge, to Messrs Greene King and Sons Ltd for £1320. The brewery also supplied the Duke of Wellington, Willingham, and the Black Horse Inns at Willingham, Over and Rampton, all of which were included in the auction sale.

A Baptist Sunday School outing

When this Baptist Sunday School outing was held in the 1890s, a man carrying a red flag had to walk in front of motorised vehicles to slow down their speed. He can be seen in the foreground with his flag. This law was very unpopular, not least with the men carrying the flags! The annual London to Brighton Run was started to celebrate the repeal of the legislation in 1896.

The fire engine, which was bought for £85 in 1790

The Fire Engine House showing its dilapidated state c1900

The Fire Engine House in 1936

The village pump and the Fire Engine House are on the left, and in the background, the Salvation Army Band can be seen playing outside their meeting hall. The playing followed their regular Sunday evening service, which was held near to the Victoria Lamp. The village sign later replaced the lamp.

The Salvation Army Hall to the Three Horseshoes Public House

Access to the Salvation Army barn, before the hall was built, was through a gate in the wall on the left.

The Salvation Army first came to Cottenham in January 1886, when Alice Copsey and Susan Sindall hired the British School Room (the Margett Street School) for meetings.

This popular rhyme was sung:

> *In 1886 the Salvation Army to Cottenham came*
> *Alice Copsey and Susan Sindall by name*
> *People said they would surely fall*
> *But GLORY HALLELUJAH they conquered ALL!*

There was some opposition to their open-air meetings on Todd's Corner on the junction of Telegraph Street and the High Street, and at the corner of Lambs Lane and the High Street. There were still well over twenty public houses in the village, and an 'Anti-Salvation Army Tea' was organised at the Hopbind. Constable Vialls, the village policeman, suggested the lasses go back to Cambridge for their own safety.

A 'Flying Squad of Hallelujah Lasses' was sent from Cambridge later in the year. They used several buildings, including barns in the High Street near the church and another in Telegraph Street, before they came to the 'Old Barn' behind the present hall. A band and singing company were formed, and for many years the band led the Feast Parade. Land at the front of the 'Old Barn' was purchased for a hall, which was opened on 17th July 1937.

The Salvation Army Band outside Thomas Ivatt's house in 1906

In the back row, from the left are Charles Gifford, Harry Bowers, George Fishpool, Frederick Furbank, Walter Rogers, Ben Symonds, Will Fowler, Frank Kidman, Henry Bennerson, James Emerson, Jack Tibbett, James Kidman, and George Trundley. In the front row are Arthur Trundley, Percy Webb, John Bowers, Mr Jackson, Richard Croxon and James Trundley.

A marvellous display of local produce and basketry for a Salvation Army Harvest Festival c1905

185 High Street – Mitchell House

This photograph shows Mr and Mrs Goode in their carriage. Their coachman was Charles Rayner. Marmaduke Ivatt built Mitchell House in about 1847. The Ivatt family let the premises to John Morlin Goode at £35 per year from 1882 until 1904, when Mr Goode bought it for £2,400. Mr Goode pulled down a house that stood where the Topiary Tree shop is now sited to build a wall all around the site. Ben Watson worked for the builder, Mr Young of Lambs Lane, on the wall construction. He remembers when the job was nearly complete Mr Goode enquired about progress. 'Nearly there, Mr Goode. We're on the last course now', replied the men. At this point a pedestrian passed by on the road and, seeing Mr Goode in his garden, greeted him, 'Good morning, Mr Goode'. 'Good morning', replied Mr Goode, immediately turning to the builders, saying 'Put another foot or two on the top!'

Mrs Goode as a young woman

Mrs Goode, who died in 1932, left over £153,000 in her will. The largest bequest was made to the old Addenbrookes Hospital; a ward was later named Goode in recognition of her generosity. Mrs Goode was the daughter of John Swan, auctioneer and cabinet-maker, whose premises were at 18-19 Sidney Street Cambridge.

Mitchell House was sold in the midst of the depression in 1933 for just £1,400 to James De Graaff Hunter.

1st Cottenham Guides

The 1st Cottenham Guides are shown with Lady Brackenbury in the grounds of Mitchell House in 1944-45. In the back row, from the left are Sheila Badcock, Stella Read, Joy Ward, Pam Simpkins, Iris Thulborn, Maisie Young and Marlene Watson. In the middle row are Hilary Addison, Jeanette Watson, Joyce Edwards, Lady Brackenbury, Ethel Murfitt, Vivienne Webb and Hope Symonds. At the front are Joan Thulborn and Audrey Smith.

Browns of Gwydir Street, Cambridge

Browns of Gwydir Street, Cambridge, came every week with their stock of household goods. The first photograph is taken opposite Margett Street, where the Fire Station is now sited. The second photograph was taken when Browns became motorised.

Another regular visitor to the village was Mr Silvester of East Road, Cambridge, who sold ice cream in the village on Saturday evenings before the Second World War. He would call out 'Okey Cokey, all's nice I've got, anybody else please?' He had a large container of ice cream floating in water and ice. It was the best ice cream around, but he never disclosed the recipe, and it was lost when he died.

160 High Street
Clifford Norman, on the left, operating an asparagus bundling machine c1905. The other people shown are Mrs Newman Chapman, Mrs Charles Smith, May Moule, Mrs Webb and Alfred Sanderson. Raffia (also known as bass) or thin willow was used to tie the asparagus in bundles of 50 or 100.

This extraordinary charabanc, with hard tyres, was hired for the Baptist outing to Clacton in 1923.

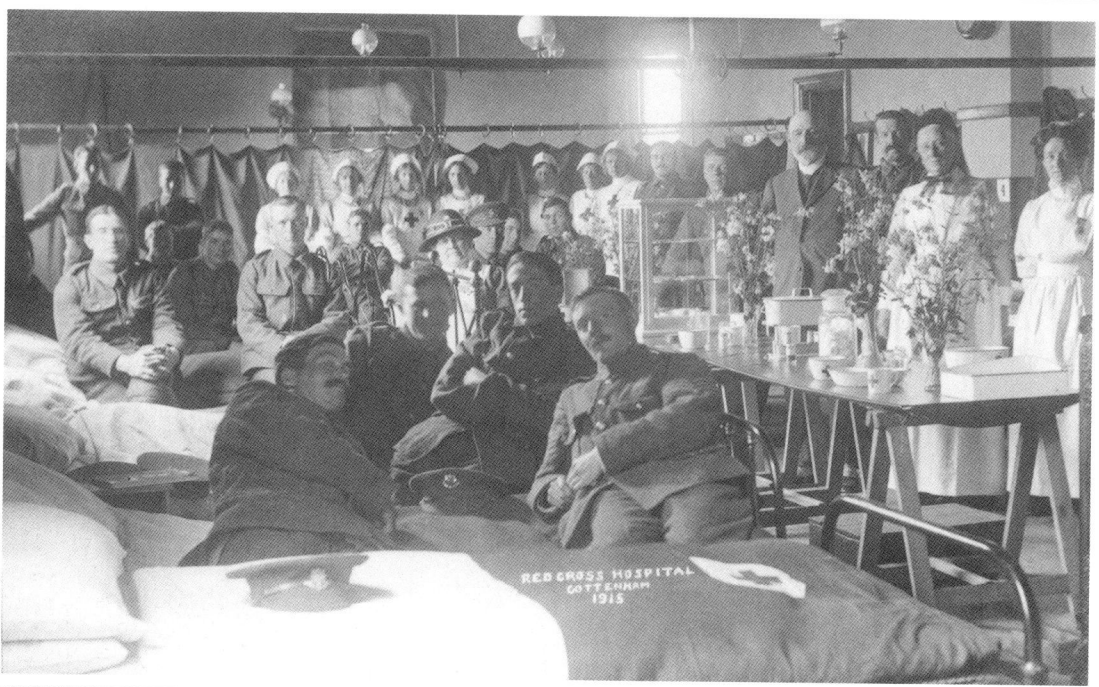

The Baptist Chapel

The Cambridge V.A.D. (Voluntary Aid Detachment) Hospital Number 36 mobilised at Cottenham on Friday 14th May 1915. Twenty patients were received at the Baptist Chapel Schoolroom. A bathroom containing a bath with hot and cold water was added in December 1916, at a time when few houses in the village had such facilities. The Chapel Deacons asked the Red Cross to leave on 5th October 1917 after the occupants were discovered dancing and playing cards on the premises. The patients were subsequently accommodated at the Rectory.

A rook shooting party setting off for Denny Abbey from the V.A.D. Hospital in the Baptist Chapel. The King's Head public house can be seen at the far left of the photograph.

A donation of food for old Addenbrookes Hospital
In October 1919 the Cottenham Feast Parade Committee collected fruit and vegetables on this Lack & Sons steam lorry. The produce was then taken to the old Addenbrookes Hospital. There were 87 bags of potatoes, 10 bags of carrots, and 75 bushels of apples.

Kathleen Smith, May Smith, Edith Raven and Queenie Collins on their way to the Baptist Sunday School Anniversary Egg and Flower Service in the late 1920s.

Mrs Josiah Smith's Bible Class at the Baptist Chapel in the early 1900s
From the left in the back row are May Rayment, Etty Moore, Florence Gautrey, Agnes Hart, Winnie Allen, unknown, Edith Leader and Cissie Moore. In the middle row are unknown, Edith Collins, Mrs Josiah Smith, Ethel Fishpool, and Miss Todd. In the front row are Charlotte Moule, Gertie Chivers and unknown.

145 High Street
There were three small shops on the corner of Rooks Street. From the corner, these were William Carter the shoemaker, Jimmy Moore the barber and John Burgess the butcher.

135 High Street - The Three Horseshoes in 1900

Probably built after the great fire of 1676, the Three Horseshoes was one of the earliest of the licensed houses in Cottenham, one of the most popular and at times, doing the best trade.

Calf sales were held at the Three Horseshoes until c1870. The drovers had large pots of ale and in order that the calves' tails and halters should not knock the pots from the tables or trestles, the custom of 'ugging' arose. The pot was hugged to the body in the crook of the arm. The terms 'ugging' and 'Gulpers' were associated with Cottenham.

Two large ground and first floor rooms, measuring 32ft x 17ft, were added to the house in 1873. When the property was sold by auction in 1895 it was described as: 'The well situated public house the Three Horseshoes occupied by Messrs Apthorpe & Son and their undertenant'. It was sold to the Norwich brewers Bullard and Sons for £545.

Several groups held their meetings in the large rooms of this public house. The Manchester Unity Friendly Society was 'a beneficial and educational order for men, women and children' which offered insurance benefits for sickness, old age and death. Another Friendly Society meeting here, at least until 1926, was the Loyal Order of Ancient Shepherds (Ashton Unity). The Loyal Princess Alexandra Lodge held meetings at the Three Horseshoes on every 4th Monday of the month.

Until 1925, a ploughmen's dinner was held here following the annual ploughing match. The Three Horseshoes also hosted functions for the Cottenham football and cricket clubs, notable guests being officers of the Metropolitan Police Force.

The house was closed in 1967 and is currently undergoing restoration.

Between 135 and 139 High Street - Whitehead's Bicycle Factory

The Whitehead Factory yard

A view in the workshop, with George Whitehead at the front
The workshop operated from 1886 until around the time of the First World War. Many cycling champions rode a Whitehead's Senior Wrangler, including Sidney Lack.

An advertisement for 'Gentlemen's Bicycles'

An advertisement for 'Motor Bicycles'

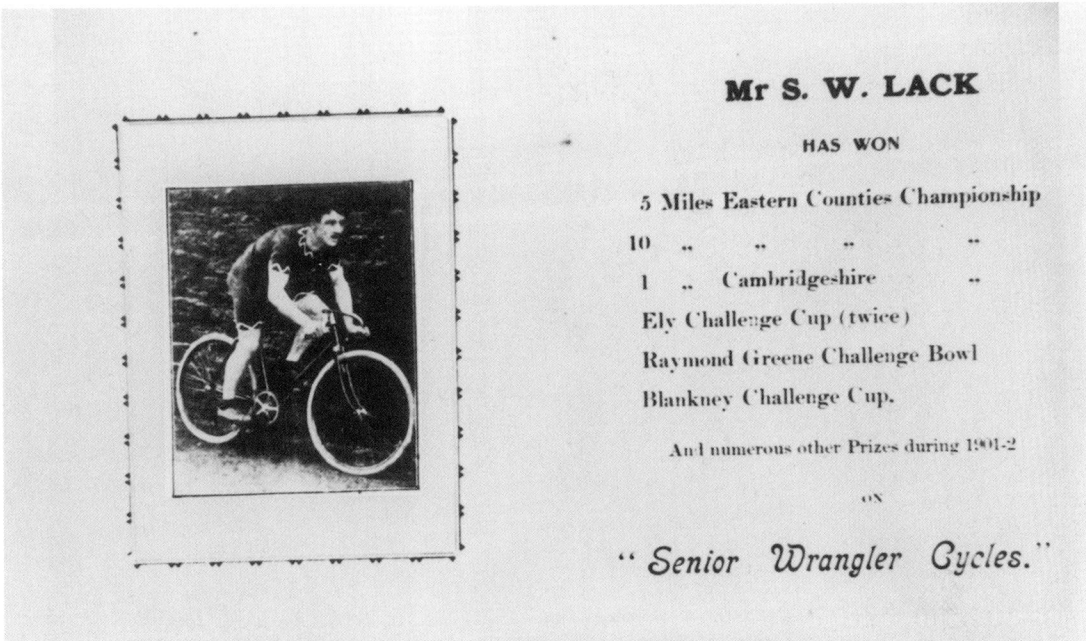

An advertisement showing Sidney Lack

Sidney Lack's prizes

During the 1901-02 season, on the day Sidney Lack won the Ely Challenge Cup, he first cycled fifteen miles to Ely, via Landbeach, in the slipstream behind two other Cottenham cyclists. Following the afternoon race at Ely he rode back to Cambridge, in the slipstream behind the Cottenham cyclists again, and won a championship in Cambridge! This was a great achievement, especially considering the poor condition of the roads at the time.

At about the same time, another Cottenham cyclist, John Lee, was winning races on his Senior Wrangler bicycle. He is shown here with Arthur Maskell and his prizes.

A Whitehead's bicycle, with a buckled front wheel, having been run over by a tumbril cart

121 High Street – The Royal British Legion to the Church

The British Legion

The first Cottenham Post Office opened in the Pepys School (which later housed the Royal British Legion) on Monday 2nd October 1843, when Mr Thomas Haird was master at the school. A postman walked out from Cambridge in the morning, with letters for Histon and Cottenham, returning at about four o'clock in the afternoon. This was only three years after Sir Roland Hill's system of uniform penny postage had begun.

The Pepys School was built in 1835 to replace the school first established before 1596 near the church. The first school was destroyed in 1617 when the steeple fell onto it, and was rebuilt with an endowment by Katherin Pepys in 1697. Katherin Pepys had left money for a school to educate twenty-one poor charity boys. When the new Pepys School was built at 121 High Street, about seventy boys could be accommodated. Free education was limited to twenty-six boys; the other forty-four boys were fee-paying pupils. Arguments arose because the rector and church-wardens decided which children could attend. Dissenters in the village therefore built the school in Margett Street, which subsequently became the Board School. The Pepys School closed in 1880.

An evening class at the Pepys School building

Evening classes were a part of village life before the turn of the twentieth century. The Brass and Bent Ironwork class was held in the former Pepys School between 1890 and 1900. The photograph includes the teacher Fred Stone, Thomas Haird, Fred Smith and Benjamin Moore.

Children from the Margett Street School later used the room for cookery and woodwork classes.

The Royal British Legion occupied the building from 1923; the recreational facilities included billiards, a popular sport in the village.

120 High Street - Pond Farm

A group of fifty dissenting families, which called itself 'The Church Congregation Society of the Protestant Dissenters of the Denomination of Independence', worshipped in the barn behind this 17th century farmhouse.

A chapel was then built in 1781 on the same site as the current Baptist Chapel. The first minister of the chapel, Thomas Baron, was a Baptist so the Society subsequently became part of the Baptist movement. The Toleration Act of 1689 had allowed freedom of worship to those who could not accept the teaching of the Anglican Church.

Pond Farm was also the site for meetings of the Ranters, or Primitive Methodists, in the 19th century before their own chapel was built by Matthew Moore at 138 High Street, c1860. The Primitive Methodist Chapel later became a fish shop, a Home Guards store during the Second World War, and then the Labour Hall. It is now the Rosary Nursery.

This photograph with Pond Farm in the background was taken in 1931 when Mrs Elizabeth A. Goode presented a new standard to the Royal British Legion.

The Broad Lane pond was filled in during 1930. This photograph shows the pond with a hayrick in the Pond Farm rickyard in the background.

115-117 High Street – Pond and Victoria Villas

These villas were built in 1902 on the site where Robert Norman's house and bakery had previously stood. Robert died on 30th August 1746, leaving about ten thousand pounds, and it is said he accumulated this money by 'industry and thrift'. He had continued going to Cambridge market every Saturday until shortly before he died, but, according to the diary entry of William Coles of Milton, would allow himself no refreshment, 'not so much as to alight off his horse for fear of an expense that would attend to it, but went back again as soon as his business was done. I saw him, with amazement, in February last at Cambridge on an excessively cold and bleak day which he bid defiance to when one of his sons, who was with him, would willingly have got under shelter had his father permitted it'.

The white house, with its bakery, was sold to the Clarke family in the 1870s and then sold again in *c*1898 to Arthur Moore, who had made his fortune in London. It is said that Arthur Moore left the village to work in a London public house as a potboy. He prospered and eventually owned the Coach and Horses public house on the Clapham Road! He built the two new houses, believed to be the last houses in the village constructed from Cottenham brick. His brother William Moore lived in the right-hand house, and Kimpton Moore lived and worked in the left-hand house. Note the baker's shop to the right side of the house on the left. The new bakery was sited at the rear of the house and Harry Moore carried on the business until June 1954.

108-110 High Street

The Moreton's Charity built the Church End Almshouses on this site in 1816. There were two rows of almshouses with a communal washhouse in the centre and a row of outside toilets. Each front door was shared by two almshouses. Aged widows and elderly men, most of whom were in receipt of parochial relief, inhabited them.

Moreton's Charity was one of several charities established by benefactors to Cottenham before there was adequate public provision for care of the poor. On 26th August 1671, John Moreton set up a charity with eight trustees (with four coming from London and four from Cottenham) to distribute the income from property called Liquor Pond field, near Gray's Inn Lane, St Andrews, Holborn. The Trustees were to place poor Cottenham children as apprentices and to give out poor relief, according to the advice of the church-wardens of Cottenham. The Trustees offered their accounts to the minister or curate annually on St John's Day.

In 1837, in their *Report of the Commissioners for Enquiring Concerning Charities*, the Commissioners noted the income of over £200 per year was distributed 'in putting out apprentices, and in the relief of the poor in coal tickets and money gifts of about £1 each in time of illness and need'. The almshouses were reported to be in good repair. At this time the local Trustees were Messrs T. Hall, W. Sanderson, James Graves and Ivatt O. Cross.

One of the almshouse tenants, Alf Rich, who is remembered because he used to say, 'If we can't have bread, we'll have toast'.

109 High Street - King Smith's cottage
John Smith bought the white house in 1744, and it remained with the same family until 1973.

102 High Street

The workhouse was originally on this site, remaining until after the Poor Law Amendment Act of 1834, when the poor of Cottenham had to go to the workhouse in Union Lane, Chesterton, Cambridge. The site was sold in 1840 to James Chivers, who built the house.

Herbert Male, the butcher, added bay windows to the house in about 1900 to allow extra light into the front rooms. Three of his children had consumption, and it was thought better lit rooms would be beneficial. Sadly, Selena, Clara and Lizzie succumbed to the disease anyway. Mr Male's shop is the black wooden building to the left of the house. It closed in 1932.

105 High Street

Four generations of the Benton family had lived in the house, seen on the far right of the photograph, before it was demolished in 1956.

101-103 High Street

Three generations of the Rowell family owned the house second from the right from 1774 to 1892. In 1854, John Rowell and his family emigrated to Adelaide, South Australia, where they settled down to become fruit, nut and vegetable growers. Several descendants became distinguished soldiers. One son, Lieutenant Colonel James Rowell, led the South Australian Mounted Rifles Honour Guard in the London procession at Queen Victoria's Diamond Jubilee.

89 High Street

The Woods family owned the house to the left of the thatched barn from 1768. Thomas Woods and his wife went to America in 1881 in order to escape their debts. They arranged to sell their horses to a Swaffham Prior dealer at Waterbeach Station as they left. Brittain Diddell, the harness maker, on hearing the Woods had fled, rode after them for the money they owed him, but the train had already departed. Mr Diddell went to a choral meeting that evening, where he collapsed and died, due no doubt to stress. The mortgagee foreclosed on the property and Ephraim Gautrey settled the debt. The Gautrey family still own the property.

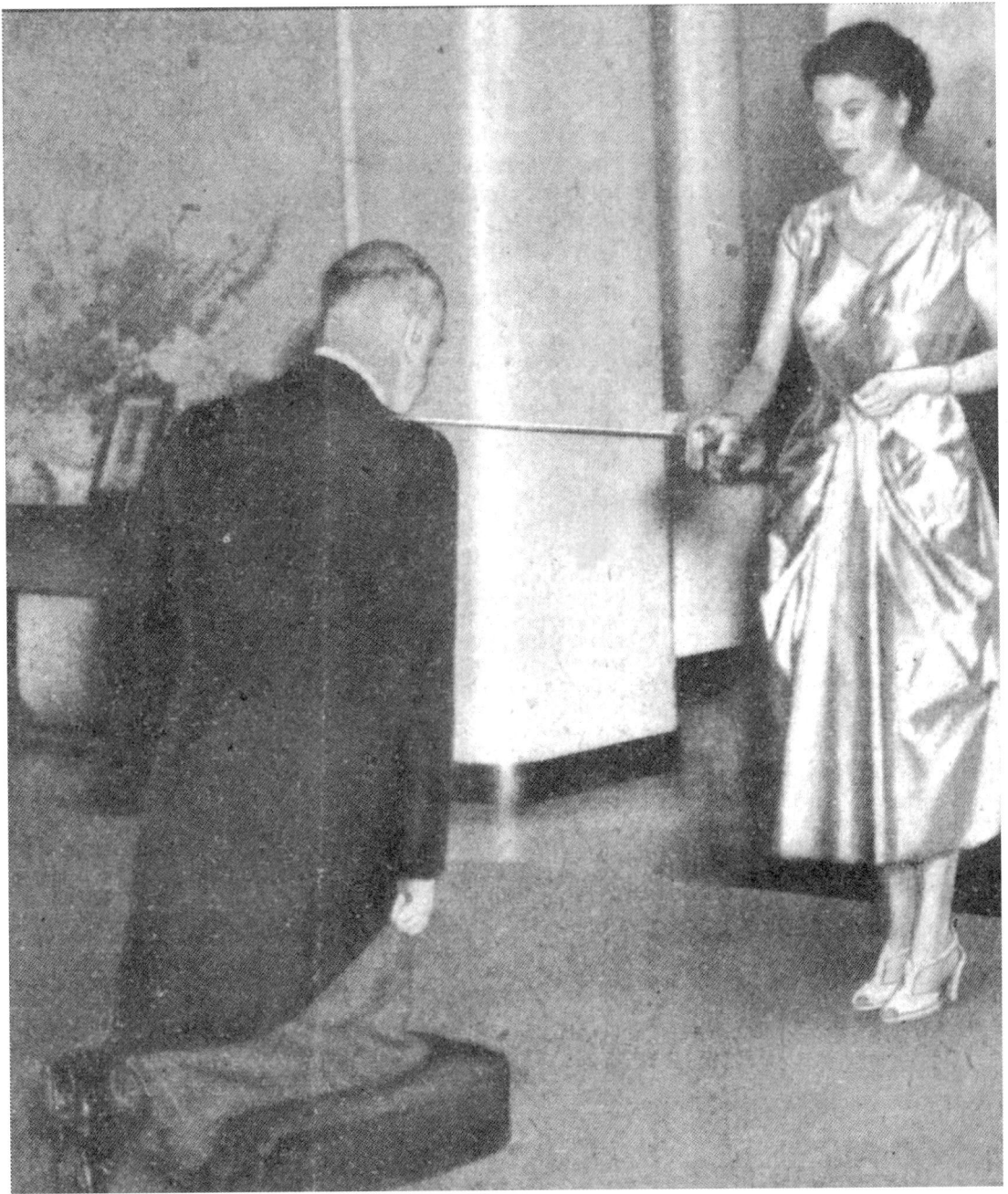

A Cottenham descendant is knighted

James Rowell's son, Sydney Fairbairn Rowell, served at Gallipoli. He remained in the forces until he retired as Chief of the Australian General Staff in 1954. The photograph shows him being invested as Knight Commander of the Order of the British Empire by the Queen in February 1954, after she opened the Parliament in Canberra.

85 High Street

This was the house of Fred Stone, watch and clockmaker, local photographer and music teacher. Mr Stone also ran an evening class at the Pepys School. He had come from Hastings and married Lizzie Cross who owned this old farmhouse. Fred altered it to make a shop in the front right hand corner, as is evident in this photograph.

In the background, the old Jolly Millers public house can be seen; it burnt down in 1898.

A wedding party

On 17th April 1911 Henry William Smith, aged twenty-one, son of publican Ernest Smith, married Lily Violet Sprawton, aged twenty-one, daughter of Josiah Sprawton of Godmanchester at Cottenham Church. The photograph was taken at the rear of 85 High Street, the home of Fred Stone the photographer.

72 High Street – Ingle's Workshop, photographed in 1900

David Ingle was a carpenter and undertaker in a business established by his forebears in the early 1830s. From the left are Sidney Ingle, David Ingle, Aaron Rayment and Mr Fox.

70 High Street

Murfitt's the watchmaker operated at this address from 1846 to 1920.

Next to the property was Charles Kilburn's butcher's shop. He sold 'foreign' meat, principally chilled meat from New Zealand, but this innovation was not popular!

John Ivatt owned the brickyards at the bottom of Ivatt Street and lived in the house to the right of Ivatt Street. Mr Ivatt was blind, so he had the cobbles installed to help him feel his way across the street. He was in very little danger from traffic!

Supplying water to Church End

Ezra Lee is shown holding the reins of the water cart and his two sons, Reginald and Francis, are in the goat cart. Mrs Lee is at the rear of the water cart and the other people pictured are family friends.

The water cart was filled from the pump on the Green to provide water for the houses at Church End. Buckets, which were left outside the houses, were filled four times a week in 1902.

Well water at Church End was declared unfit to drink following a typhoid epidemic in 1885. Water was carted in this way until a piped water supply was laid in 1903. The cost of the water cart was borne by the parish.

39 High Street

This property was used as a bus garage between the First and Second World Wars. It housed the last bus from Cambridge at night, which would leave again at 7.10 a.m. the next day.

44 High Street

Bartingales' House, the thatched house on the left, was typical of farmhouses built in Cottenham after the 1676 fire. There were three rooms along the street on the ground floor. The parlour and kitchen were built either side of the chimney, with a dairy to the side. There were two bedrooms and a cheese room above. The cheese room usually had a lattice window and was open to the thatch.

In 1928 the last family member, Miss Eliza Bartingale, who was acting strangely, was taken to Fulbourn Asylum Hospital. It was claimed that there was no money for her upkeep, so the authorities decided to sell the house and contents. When they were clearing the house, they found £122 attached to the bedding, which would have been more than enough for her care. The sale went ahead, regardless of the find, so that when she was discharged some weeks later, there was nowhere for her to go. Even some of her clothes had been sold. She was so distressed that she had to return to the hospital!

King's farmhouse, 31 High Street, built by King's College in 1861, is opposite Bartingales' house, and then comes Bernards, the home of Arthur Bull, the fruit-grower and local historian. Bernards was known as 'Blind Miss Bulls' house' as three of Mr Bull's five daughters were born blind.

On the left in the background, a small, white cottage can be seen. This was the home of the ancestors of Calvin Coolidge, American President from 1923 to 1929. Descendants of the Coolidge family, who left for Massachusetts in 1630, still visit the village.

Note that is was safe for children to play cricket on the street!

13 High Street, photographed in 2002

In 1624 John Haddow, as a copyholder of the Rectory Manor, sold his messuage (an old term for a house, with its gardens, yard, orchard and outbuildings) at 13 High Street, and 5 roods at Smithy Fen, for £40. The transaction took place in the south porch of the church.

Later, when Francis Wisdom died in 1681, this property passed to his living daughter, Edith Matthews, and John Dimmock, the son of his deceased daughter. The house was still under split ownership when it was substantially altered in 1723. Brick walls were added and the roof was rebuilt, partly thatched and partly tiled to show the division of ownership. In 1759, Richard Matthews, Edith's son, who already owned the part nearest the church, bought the other part, and returned the house to one property again.

11 High Street
These ladies were celebrating the Relief of Mafeking in May 1900. It must have been difficult cycling on this road surface. To the right is a shop known as Little Selfridges. Two elderly spinsters, Miss Agnes Cross, and her companion, Miss Clara Smith, ran it. If you rang the bell, one of them would appear from behind a curtain to serve you. Miss Smith was known as 'Kisser Smith' as she had a habit of kissing children.

5 High Street, the original Wheatsheaf public house
The present house was built behind the old house, which was still able to continue trading during the building project.

The Parish Church of All Saints, Cottenham

A postcard showing All Saints Parish Church c1952

The earliest evidence of a church on this site is from the mid-tenth century. A charter from King Edred confirming Turketel's benefaction to Crowland Abbey mentions a church in Cottenham in 948. There must have been a Norman building too, as there are some pieces of Norman zigzag moulding embedded in the south chancel wall. The existing church was built in the Perpendicular style of the 15th century, but has undergone major alterations ever since. The woodwork is mainly Victorian. The oak pews were installed in 1867 by the local craftsman Jonathan Haird, though two London men did the carvings on the pew ends. These woodcarvers were occupied for about nine months copying local flowers, fruit and foliage gathered by the daughters of the rector, Samuel Banks.

The church tower, with its distinctive ogee pinnacles, stands about 100 feet high. It was built on the base of the 15th century steeple which was destroyed in a gale in 1617. It was originally cased in stucco, which was removed in 1928. In addition to the weather vane, and the clock on the west side, there is a sundial with the inscription 'The time is short' on the south side of the tower.

Over the centuries, All Saints Parish Church has been associated with several clergymen who subsequently had distinguished careers. Robert de Orford (rector from 1310) became Bishop of Ely and Laurence Bothe (rector from 1444) became Lord Chancellor and Archbishop of York. William Warham was rector from 1501. As Archbishop of Canterbury he officiated at the marriage of Henry VIII and Katherine of Aragon on 3rd June 1509. Leonard Mawe (rector from 1623) became Bishop of Bath and Wells.

John Tenison had a more modest, but perhaps more remarkable career. He was curate of Cottenham from 1624 to 1673, during which period he served six rectors, including Dr John Manby, whose story is told later. He served throughout a very unsettled period of British history. Charles I became King of England in 1625, and ruled without Parliament from 1629. The King was forced by bankruptcy to recall Parliament in 1640. This became the Long Parliament that continued to sit until 1660, through the English Civil War (1642-49), the execution of Charles I, and the establishment of the Commonwealth in 1649.

Oliver Cromwell was Lord Protector of the Commonwealth from 1653 to 1658. The Long Parliament dissolved itself in March 1660, and the Stuart monarchy was restored in May 1660 when Charles II was crowned. The Great Plague struck in 1665.

Throughout this troubled time, churches were shut, or used as stables, barracks or fortresses. No records of local baptisms were kept between 1637 and 1641, and the Bishop of Ely was imprisoned in the Tower of London for eighteen years. John Tenison sent his son Thomas, born in Cottenham in 1636, away to school in Norwich. Thomas then came to Cambridge to study medicine at Corpus Christi College, Cambridge, but was ordained after the Restoration of the Monarchy. He remained in Cambridge during the Great Plague, attending his parishioners, while most of his colleagues fled. He became Archbishop of Canterbury in 1694. He crowned Queen Anne in 1702 and King George I in 1714. Thomas Tenison died in 1715.

The interior of All Saints Church, showing the screen

A panoramic view of the Old Rectory and Smithy Fen taken from All Saints Church tower

The Old Rectory was built in several stages from the late 16th century. It replaced a medieval rectory, said to have fallen into extreme ruin by 1538.

The rector from 1635 was Dr John Manby. He is said to have been 'a man of unblemished piety, of considerable learning and benevolent in his parish', but at the height of Puritan extremism he came to the notice of the Parliamentary Commissioner, the Duke of Manchester. Dr Manby was found guilty of 'scandalous crimes' such as restoring the communion table to the east end of the church, reading the Communion Service, and bowing to the holy table. Early in 1641, he was imprisoned in St John's College, Cambridge, which had been converted into a temporary gaol. Dr Manby escaped to Middleton-on-the-Wolds in Yorkshire in 1645, but was turned away from this village twelve months later. He returned to Cottenham, where dramatic events had occurred in the meantime at the rectory.

In 1644 the rectory was given to Oliver Cromwell's sister, Robina. The local historian, Arthur Bull, recorded in the March 1899 edition of the Parish Magazine, that she 'shortly afterwards bestowed both it and herself upon Peter French', who became the next rector. While Dr Manby was imprisoned, Mrs Manby had remained in the rectory until a 'band of soldiers, under the command of Major Jordan, the Governor of Cambridge Castle, proceeded to Cottenham, and having entered the rectory with their pistols cocked and swords drawn, turned Mrs Manby out of doors into the road, with her five small children, the youngest being a baby in arms. The corn and cattle had already been seized'. Mrs Manby took refuge with Dr Manby's sister, Hester Cass, who lived in Cottenham, and remained with her for eighteen months, despite considerable harassment. When Dr Manby returned to his family in Cottenham, he was arrested, along with his sister, and taken to gaol in London. He was never again brought to trial, and was eventually released from prison. He ran a small private school for a time in London, but remained dependent on his family until he was reinstated to his living at Cottenham in 1660.

The house was sold into private ownership in 1964 and a new rectory was built in the grounds to the south.

A tea party on the Rectory Lawn, c1900

Cottenham Girls' Drilling Class with the Reverend Greig in the Rectory Garden on Whit Monday 1901
In the back row are the instructor Mrs Arthur Sargeant, May Clarke, Grace Maskell, unknown, Nora Ansell, Clara Male, Edith Leader, Annie Leader and Maud Smith.

In the third row are the curate Edmundson Webb, Mabel Rowell, Lottie Graves, unknown, Etty Lee, unknown, Miss Collins, unknown, Florrie Emerson, Louisa Greig, Mrs Atkinson and Mrs Albert Sargeant.

In the second row are Miss Greig, Mrs Webb, unknown, M. Camps, Miss Carter, unknown, unknown, unknown, Ethel Smith, Mrs Greig and the Reverend David Greig.

In the front row are Miss Ely, unknown, Harry Sargeant, the curate's daughter, Cedric Sargeant, unknown and Miss Haird.

Cottenham Church Gymnasium Club

The pre-First World War Cottenham Church Gymnasium Club with instructor Herbert Carter, standing in the middle of the group. This was held at the Church Schoolroom every Monday. From the back left to back right, the gymnasts are Percy Milton, Fred Peck, Sidney Pratt, Ernest Thulbourn, Harry Smith, Mr Leete, Tom Ely, Arthur Pierson, Percy Carter, Frank Sanderson, William Wilkin, Antony Maskell, Sidney Carter, and William Taylor.

The Old Church Hall

The Church Hall was built by the Reverend Banks and his family as an Industrial School for Girls. The first brick was laid by his eldest daughter in May 1852. The twenty-five pupils were to learn cookery and needlework, as this type of instruction was all that girls needed!

Mr William Coles' brother, from Church Close, with a full cartload of bread

The bake house was built by Gabriel Smith in the 1880s, and shortly afterwards was taken over by Havelock Clarke, and then by William Coles. The Coles family ran the business until 1961.

The cottages on the churchyard wall were pulled down in 1930 when the last resident, Arthur 'Dick' Hyam, moved into a new council house on Twentypence Road.

Twentypence Road

Twentypence derives its name from a parcel of thirty acres of land with this name on the Cottenham side of the river. It was described in Richard Atkins' *Survey of the Fens* in 1604.

The Church End pump on Twentypence Road

There were four public pumps in Cottenham: at the Green, at Garibaldi Terrace, at Lordship Lane and below the rectory at Church End. The Church End pump was erected in 1864, and was supplied with water from Cottenham Lode, known locally as 'the cut', by a pipe laid across Rectory Paddock; there was also a water trough for the animals. Three of the pumps were removed in 1955, leaving the last remaining pump in place at Church End. This photograph was taken shortly before the Village Society moved it to the Green in 1985.

The drawbridge

There had been several methods of crossing the river before the bridge was built over the Great Ouse (or Old West River) in 1931, at a cost of £8,000.

Until c1907 there was a type of ferry, known as a drawbridge, which was attached by chains on either side of the river. A brewer's dray, which supplied public houses in the Wilburton area from Peck's brewery at the Hopbind public house until 1904, crossed the river on this drawbridge. Dr Cox and his daughter Ethel (who was later to become Mrs Ellis) are shown in the photograph.

A view across the river at Twentypence

Crossing the river 1907-31
After the drawbridge was removed, you had to shout for the bargeman Albert Savage, who lived in the cottage across the road from the public house. The punt was almost always on the other side of the river!

Exploring the Side Streets of Cottenham

In this chapter, we travel back through the village from Church End, exploring the streets to the north west, the 'Lanes' to the south east and the roads to the south of the High Street.

Ivatt Street to Tenison Manor

The cottages in Ivatt Street

These twelve terraced cottages cost £660 in 1865 when John Ivatt built them. Initially, the cottages had two rooms up and two rooms down; there was no drainage and the toilets were at the bottom of the yard. A water tap was installed on the High Street at the top of the lane after the supply was laid in 1903. There were eighty-three people living in Ivatt Street in 1891.

The street was known locally as Brickle Lane because in 1830, John Ivatt had founded a brick works at the bottom of the lane. When he died in 1869 aged seventy-seven, his great-nephew, a young lad also named John Ivatt, inherited the property. The younger John Ivatt became an ironmonger at New Southgate and James Ely and his sons managed the brickworks. The works ceased operation before a final sale of stock in 1908, when competition from larger mechanised brickworks made the production of the local hand-made bricks uneconomical. The brick pits are still evident.

4 Broad Lane - Oasland House, photographed in 2002

After the Toleration Act, granted by King William in 1689, the nonconformists openly formed themselves into a separate church at Cottenham. The Reverend Oasland, who lived at this house until he died in 1711, established the church in 1694. He is buried at Oakington.

On the right of Broad Lane, approximately where Males Close is situated, is an area known as Church Hill. A local legend states that when the Saxon lord wanted to build a church on this site, the Devil used to come by night and move the stones down to the end of the village. The Devil was so persistent that eventually the local people conceded defeat, and built the church on its current site. Richard Mortimer, the archaeologist involved with the Tenison Manor excavation, believes that such legends often have a basis in truth. He considers that it was quite likely there was a Saxon church on this site, as it was close to the manor, even though no physical evidence has been found to date. It is very unlikely that the Saxon church would have been sited at All Saints Church as it would have been too far from the Saxon village.

Tenison Manor, photographed in 2002

Children in the village took part in a competition to decide the name of the housing estate. 'Tenison' comes from Thomas Tenison, who was Archbishop of Canterbury from 1694 to 1715. The epithet 'Manor' comes from the Crowland Manor, upon which the estate is built. The streets have been named after the various birds native to the area.

The construction of Tenison Manor in the late 1990s provided an opportunity for archaeologists to look for physical evidence of the very beginnings of the village of Cottenham. Whilst there is a small amount of evidence, such as pieces of pottery, of human activity within the bounds of Cottenham in the Mesolithic period (middle Stone Age), the Bronze Age, the Iron Age and the Roman period, the extensive archaeological excavations in 1996 and 1997 suggest that Cottenham first developed as a 'nucleated village' in the Middle Saxon period.

During the 7th and 8th centuries ditches were dug and there are post-holes evident from several structures. In the latter part of the 8th century and during the 9th century the location of many of the ditches changed, so that development then seemed to be centred round a core that is probably located under the junction of Lambs Lane and the High Street. The site was abandoned for a short period in the very early years of the 11th century when it is recorded in ancient documents that the Danes pillaged and burnt Cottenham. The damaged area was rebuilt between 1017 and 1032. The manor house of Crowland was apparently built in 1032 though its location is unknown. The earliest known site for the manor house is within the moat and that site dates from the 13th century.

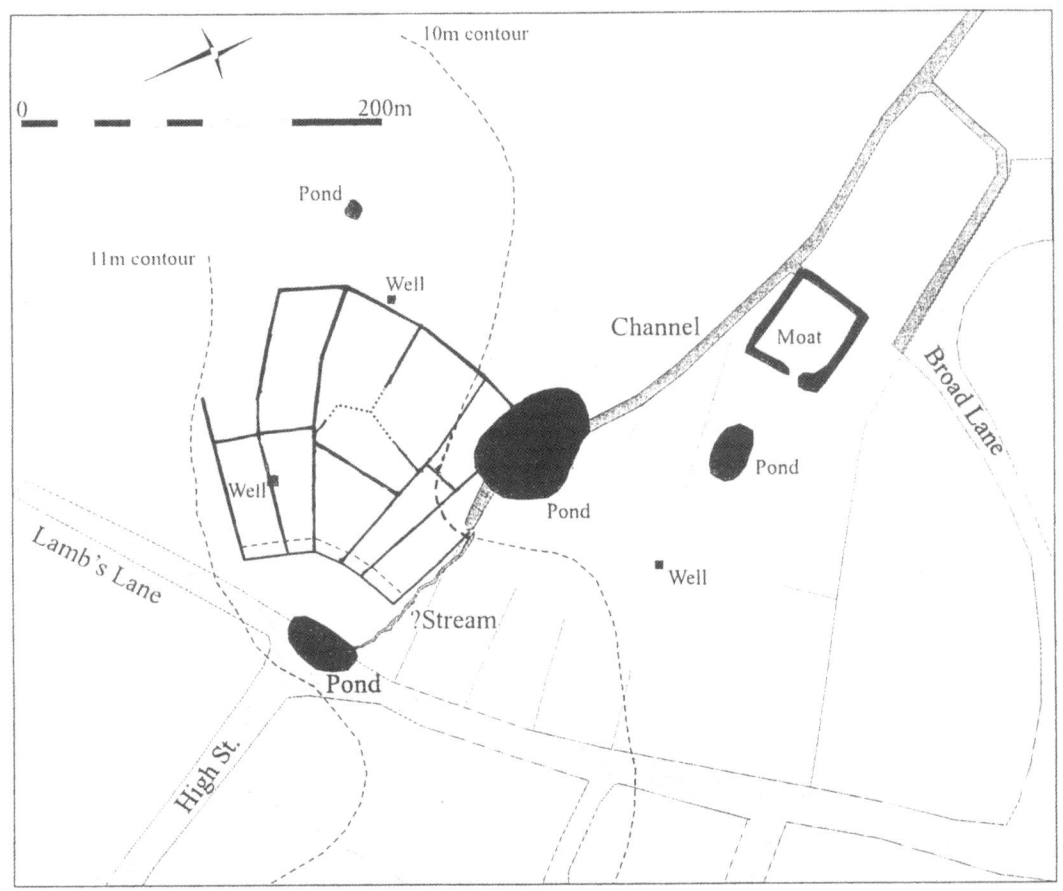

The ditches dug in the 8th and 9th centuries, and shown in bold in the diagram, suggest the shape of early Cottenham.

A pond at the corner of Lambs Lane and the High Street, which is recorded on an 1845 Enclosure Map, may mark the site of a spring or well at the centre of a Saxon village green. J.R. Ravensdale, working from documents dating from the 12th century, thought the roughly rectangular area bounded by Denmark Road, Rooks Street and the High Street was the site of the original village, but the excavations provide evidence of an earlier settlement centred on the present day road junction.

The Lanes

Traditionally, the 'Lanes' included Rooks Street, Margett Street, Corbett Street, Telegraph Street and Denmark Road. We have also included Brenda Gautrey Way.

Rooks Street

Rooks Street was known as Rooks Lane before the Enclosure. It was named after a rookery in a spinney on the church side of the lane. The present day Rooks Street was formed when a newly constructed road joined Rooks Lane over Church Field to Little End during the 1842 Enclosure. This explains its unusual shape.

The funeral of Sergeant A.W. Beaumont

Sergeant Albert William Beaumont of the Suffolk Regiment died of his wounds at Warminster on 19th December 1915, aged 39. Born in Soham, he served with the Colours for over twenty years including the South African War. He married Minnie Robertson of Cottenham in 1906. His was the first military funeral ever remembered at Cottenham. The gun-carriage with six horses accompanied by twenty-five soldiers with officers, proceeded from his home in Garibaldi Terrace along Rooks Street and the High Street to the cemetery in Lambs Lane.

Bugs Alley

These six houses were near to the corner of the High Street, on the left, and were locally known as Bugs Alley. In January 1934 the Council Surveyor, Mr Davy, said that having visited practically every part of the county, he knew of no other piece of property to compare with this from the point of view of slum conditions. The houses had no backyards or adequate air space, and one of the houses at the back of Ebenezer Chapel never received any sunlight because the alley was so narrow. There was an uncovered drain down the side of the alley and outside toilets at the rear of the chapel for the six houses. The brickwork in some of these toilets was so loose at the back that children are known to have peeped in from the yard of the King's Head public house.

An extract from the rent-book for the properties states: 'I, William Badcock, agree to rent from Mary Anne Leach a cottage situate in Rooks Lane at the weekly rent of one shilling and sixpence. I also agree to pay the water rates charged on the said cottage. Dated this 3rd day of October 1905. Signed William Badcock'.

It is said that the houses only existed until the demolition order in 1934 because Mrs F. Cross, the wife of the Chesterton Rural District Councillor for Cottenham, owned them at that time. When the houses were demolished, a Sunday School for the Ebenezer Chapel was built on the site.

Ebenezer Chapel

The Ebenezer Chapel was built following the purchase of land forty feet square from William Kimpton. The foundation stone was laid in April 1812. When gas came to Cottenham in the 1860s these lamps lit the decorative ironwork of the interior. The Ebenezer Chapel was the best-supported chapel in the village until the Second World War, but when it closed in January 1979, there were only five baptised members.

An outdoor baptism

Miss Martha Ward of the Ebenezer Baptist Chapel is shown being baptised by Pastor Morlin at Bottisham Locks in July 1901. Members of both Baptist Chapels also used the river at Lockspit Hall down Second Setchel Drove at Smithy Fen, as well as the brick-pits in Cottenham. They are known to have had to break the ice there!

The Lanes: Rooks Street

41 Rooks Street

Fred Smith, the local photographer, was the source of many of the photographs in this book. He took over Wright's General Stores in 1913 where he reputedly sold 'anything and everything'. Some of the stock in the shop when he took over the business was still for sale when he died some fifty years later. This proved to be quite handy during the Second World War when he had, for example, candles for sale when they were in short supply everywhere else.

The portraits by Fred Smith are, from the top, Elsie Barnes, Alva Burgess, and Violet Benerson.

87 Rooks Street
The Easy family has lived on this site at least since 1840. The thatched part was condemned in 1934. Susan Ferguson, stepmother of the Duchess of York, is a descendant of the Easy family.

The greengrocer's cart
Mark Beck the greengrocer used to come around the village on Saturdays. The boy is Ron Cavaliero, the lady with the bananas is Mrs Cox, and the lady to the right is Mrs Rogers.

90 Rooks Street

Village gossip suggests that when William Bedford married his second wife Nancy Cross, each believed that the other had money. When they found out neither had any, they were teased, 'Nancy diddled me, Bedford's fancy'. William Bedford built this house and shop in 1913 with a mortgage of £128. It was sold to Ernest Albert Easy, another butcher, for £625 in 1937.

The roadway between 101 and 105 Rooks Street
The Lee family lived in this house. The cottages that can be seen at the rear were known as Little End. They were approached via a pathway that is now the roadway to Fitzwilliam House. The name Little End also included that part of Rooks Street which extends to Beach Road.

98 Rooks Street
The Rose and Crown, showing Mrs Ezra Lee the wife of the licensee c1905.

125 Rooks Street

This house belonged to the Cross Family. In November 1859 John Cross kicked open the door of the Rose and Crown public house and threatened to kill ('do for') the landlady. His brother Jeremiah promised to keep him under control, but a few weeks later he was observed by Jeremiah's wife to be making his way towards the Rose and Crown, again making threats. He was thereafter confined to an upper room in the house. The thatch above his room was in such poor condition that the moon could be seen through it. In January 1862, when the weather was very cold, rumours of this state of affairs began to circulate in the village. After visits by the rector, two overseers of the parish and the doctor, John was brought downstairs suffering from hypothermia and cared for until he died a few days later. His feet had been badly frostbitten.

Garibaldi Terrace and Brenda Gautrey Way

Garibaldi Terrace fronts Beach Road and the green at Coolidge Gardens

The terrace was built in the 1860s by Thomas Piggott, a brewer from Warboys, on land formerly owned by the Cross family, and is named after the beer house that was on the corner. The beer house closed in 1894. In 1944 the whole row was sold by auction for £800.

The Garibaldi Pond, pictured on the left, was where the green is now at Coolidge Gardens. On the other side of the road is the farmyard that is now Brenda Gautrey Way. Harry Gautrey grew strawberries here; he discovered a plant that proved to be a new variety, naming it after his daughter Brenda. Although it was inclined to have a hard core, the strawberry had good flavour and became widely grown internationally as it was resistant to several diseases causing problems with strawberry yields in the 1920s. The streets off Brenda Gautrey Way are also named after varieties of locally grown strawberries – John Paxton, Royal Sovereign and King Leopold.

Denmark Road

Denmark Road was renamed in honour of Princess Alexandra, after she came to the Cottenham Races on 13th March 1870, along what had previously been known as Back Lane or Chequers Lane. In the 17th century it was also known as Wrong Street, according to Arthur Bull, the Cottenham historian. Before the Enclosure there were fewer streets in Cottenham and the fork was a major intersection in the village. The High Street from this point was known as Church Street, as it led to the church. Wrong Street just led to the fields and was therefore the wrong way to go on a Sunday morning! The name Wrong Lane was also used in *A Report of the Commissioners for Enquiring Concerning Charities* regarding purchase of a house known as 'Owisley' in 1632 for Hobson's Charity. This house is now called Ely Cottage.

56 Denmark Road

The Saintey family lived in this house for three generations until 1923, when it was sold to the Todd family. Harry Todd lived in the house. The single storey barn in the photograph was demolished to build a house for Phyllis and Clement Gautrey in 1923.

The grass island on Denmark Road
The only remaining evidence for this small green at the junction with Telegraph Street is the width of the road. Note the donkey cart. London Cottage is to the left of the brick wall. John Watts, who had worked as a brewer's drayman in London, built the house in 1834 although the initials on the wall are I.W.

Telegraph Street

Telegraph Street was renamed after the telegraph line was brought along the street from Beach Road to the Post Office. It was previously known as Watson's Lane.

36 Telegraph Street

George Hazel came to Cottenham in 1889 to keep a small shop in Garibaldi Terrace. He had previously worked as a tea blender for a firm of tea importers in King's Lynn and at this time cycled each weekend from King's Lynn to a public house called The Half Way House, between Stretham and Ely, where his mother lived. He moved to the shop in Telegraph Street from Garibaldi Terrace at about the turn of the 20th century. Mr Hazel advertised his own brand of tea that was specially blended for Cottenham water, based on the principle that Indian tea gave strength and Ceylon tea brought flavour to the brew. In common with many local shopkeepers, he would send a young lad to collect orders from his customers and then deliver their shopping. He left the Telegraph Street shop premises to Percy Young when he died in September 1939. Mr Young had worked with Mr Hazel from the age of fourteen. The shop finally closed in April 1973 when Value Added Tax was introduced.

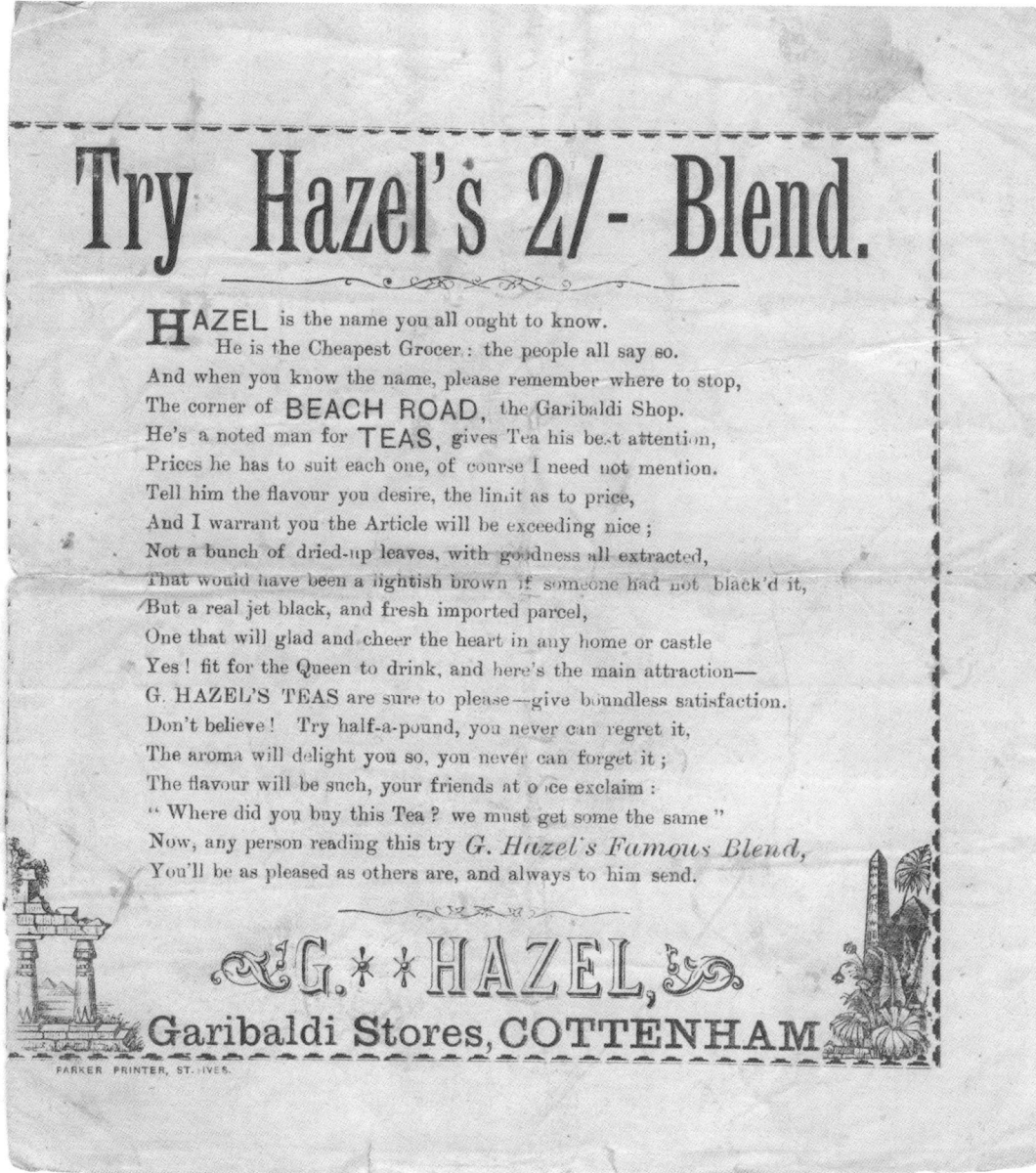

An advertisement for George Hazel's Teas

Corbett Street

In the census of 1891, Corbett Street was called Ivatt's Lane, but in the electoral roll of that year, it was known as Corbett's Lane. It was named after John Corbitt [sic], a celebrated Baptist preacher, whose family had owned property in Corbett Street around and including the Waggon and Horses. He lived in Cottenham between 1800 and 1830.

20 Corbett Street

Mrs Robert Watson and her sister Mrs Chapman made pork sausages to be sold in Cambridge at the turn of the 20th century. The sausages sold for nine pence per pound in most of Cambridge, but in the more select areas of town, the ladies charged ten pence for the same sausages!

The sisters' sausage-making machine

28-34 Corbett Street

John Lock built this row of houses. To the left, but not in the photograph, were two cottages with large overhangs of thatch where Arthur Hopkins, the mole catcher, hung his moleskins out to dry. The dried skins were sold to make protective clothing and aprons. The tenants of Locks Row objected so much to the smell that John Lock decided to buy the two cottages from the owner, 'Tiffler' Watson, demolish them and build another row of houses.

37 Corbett Street

Stanley Badcock kept this shop when he returned from military service in the First World War. Grocers were reasonably prosperous between the wars as most shopping was done locally.

Mr Badcock would take his grocery van to Oakington once a week; the local butchers offered an even more frequent service to the smaller surrounding villages.

Margett Street

Locally, Margett Street was usually known as School Lane, but was listed in old documents as Margaret's Lane. For a long period in the 18th century, Margaret Lawrence had kept a shop at the High Street end of Margett Street. She died in 1785, aged eighty. Francis Garrett suggests that Margaret's Lane was named after Mrs Lawrence. It is said that the change to the spelling occurred when a printing firm in Cambridge mistook the local pronunciation of Margaret!

The Cottenham School, Margett Street

The school was situated on land currently occupied by the library and the houses up to 28 Margett Street. The dissenters who built the first part of the school, the front hall, for a total cost of £788, opened it on 10th July 1865. The school was heated by a 'hot water apparatus' and included outside toilets and a warm place for the children who lived outside the village to eat their lunch. Local children were expected to eat at home.

It was built on the Lancastrian model, surrounded by a brick wall and iron railings and was called The British School. There were two hundred and twenty-nine children being educated at the school at the early 1870s. At this time there were also eighty boys at the Pepys School and fifty-three at the Girls' School at the church.

In these early years, regular attendance was difficult to achieve. School was not compulsory and school fees had to be paid. The government inspector gave a favourable report in 1867 but in 1869 he called at harvest time and forty children were absent.

The British School became the Board School in July 1873 and extra buildings were constructed in 1875. By 1880, the other village schools were closed and all local children went to the Margett Street School, which became a council school in 1903.

During the Second World War some of the children had to attend lessons in the church schoolroom because so many children were evacuated to the village. School dinners were first served in Cottenham in 1939, as a wartime measure, to feed the evacuee children, and the schoolroom of the Baptist Chapel on the High Street was used as the dining room.

The Ebenezer Sunday School was also used as an annexe in more recent times. The Margett Street School finally closed in 1981 when all the children had either moved across to Lambs Lane School or progressed to the Village College.

Miss Elizabeth Sutton's class in the 1880s

Mr Albert Goddard with his staff in 1895

In the back row, from the left are Miss Mary Rowell, Miss Negus, Miss Rosa Moore, Mrs Walter Smith, Miss Minnie Chivers, Miss Gertie Cross, Miss Ellen Ward, and Miss Florrie Todd.

In the middle row are Lionel Law, Miss Laura Diddell, unknown, Alfred Goddard the headmaster, unknown, Miss Edith Piggott, Miss Agnes Hart.

In the front row are the pupil teachers, Sidney Lack and Harry Cross.

At this time, teachers would train full-time in schools in a way similar to apprentices. Some of the teachers in this photograph had very long careers at the school. Miss Laura Diddell taught from 1883 to 1930 and Miss Gertie Cross taught the infants from 1888 to 1934. Other fondly remembered teachers not shown in this photograph were Miss Annie Leader, who taught from 1900 to 1950, and her cousin Miss Edith Leader, who taught from 1921 to 1947.

The Cromwell House First XI Football Team in 1935

Cromwell was one of four 'houses' which competed amongst themselves in Cottenham School. The other houses were Crowland, Pepys and Wake.

In the back row, from the left are Roy Kimpton, Bruce Currington, Malcolm Sanderson, Richard Burgess, Jack Taylor and Ronald 'Dolly' Pierson.

In the middle row are Louis Parker, Walter Scott, Mr Wiffen, Derrick Webb and Frank Ward.

In the front row are Sidney Golding, Leonard Gilbey and Leslie Barnes.

The Cottenham School First VII Netball Team in 1935

In the back row, from the left are Edith Emmans, Beryl Nielson, Freda Cornell, Audrey Male and Doris Ward.

In the front row are Nora Gautrey, Constance Currington, Mary Badcock and Gladys Simpkins.

The school's gardening class in 1928

In the back row, from the left are Ron Charlton, Ralph Thoday, Ted Barnes (from Rampton), Ken Watson, Reg Hopkins, Wally Hankin, Les Bowers, and Mr Milner, the headmaster.

In the front row are Norman Blunt, Ronald Jacklin, Frank Badcock, Harold Smith, Derek Stapleton and Cecil Rose (from Rampton).

In the background are the school poultry sheds. Sidney Ingle, who taught poultry lessons to the boys, went into considerable detail about the various breeds; it was a challenge for some of the boys to spell the breed names. Two boys were appointed to look after the hens, feed them, and record egg-laying details. Each hen had a different coloured ring on its leg. When it entered an egg-laying box, it released a wire frame that prevented it from leaving until the boys released it and recorded the details in a book. The boys were still expected to look after the hens at weekends and holidays. Sidney Ingle also taught the boys woodwork.

The headmaster, Mr Milner, is fondly remembered as a good teacher. He left Cottenham to become the founder warden of the first Village College, built at Sawston in Cambridgeshire.

Girls were also taught life skills. In the 1930s there was a large wooden building known as the Practical Room on the left-hand side of the property. The tables in this room could be adapted for the boys' woodwork or the girls' weekly lessons in cookery and laundry. For cooking, the flat tabletops were left on. The top layer would be taken off to expose the woodworking surface, with vices. Underneath this second layer were the baths for laundry. The girls had to wash the dirty laundry they had brought to school for the purpose and hang it on a long washing line in the playground. In the afternoon the clothes would be brought in, ironed and folded correctly.

In 1932 Cottenham School entered a needlework competition for schools throughout the county, organised by Eaden Lilley of Cambridge. The competition was open to girls aged eight to nine years; the task was for each girl to make a set of dolls' clothes comprising a dress, bonnet and knickers. Needlework teacher Miss Hatley so enthused the girls that all the prizes were won by four of her pupils, Nora Gautrey, Lily Badcock, Cynthia Gawthroup and Enid Collins. Headmaster Mr Milner presented the prizes and the winning entries were displayed prominently in the Market Street shop window of Eaden Lilley. The delighted pupils purchased a silver thimble for Miss Hatley to express their thanks for her skilled tuition.

Lambs Lane to Histon Road

Lambs Lane

Before the Enclosure, lambs were driven along Lambs Lane through Two Mill Field to the sheep common in Little North Fen. The sheep were taken down Broad Lane to another part of the common in North Fen. During this time Lambs Lane terminated at the Two Mill Field (which began approximately at 34 Lambs Lane).

After the Enclosure in 1842, the extension of Lambs Lane was made through the arable fields of Two Mill Field to Rampton Road and was known as Mill Road because of the tower windmill sited at the junction.

A view photographed in the early 1930s down Lambs Lane from the High Street intersection, showing the cottages built by Ellis Munsey after he bought the property in 1801. On the left are the Cottenham Supply Stores and Barclays Bank. A water pump can be seen on the extreme right.

The seat outside the Constitutional Club was brought here from the Margett Street School in 1928 when new two-seater desks were installed in the school.

1938 was a dreadful year for Cottenham as there had been a severe frost followed by a prolonged drought. At this time the population of 2,446 was largely dependent on income from the fruit and flowers grown around the village. A News Chronicle report of 22nd June 1938 stated that Charles Chivers expected to harvest only forty per cent of his normal strawberry crop and expected nothing at all from twelve acres of plums, apples, cherries and pears. 'Fruit is our very existence', said Arthur Cundell. He did not expect to need his fruit boxes that year. Local men gathered on the seat to discuss the crop failure and from this time it was known as the Cottenham Parliament.

The Cottenham Parliament
The man with the bicycle is Frank Cross. The others are, from the left, Wilson Easy, Mr Cook, Malachi Blunt, Arthur Flavel, Charlie Gifford, William Carrier and James Piper.

Village veterans around the Victoria Lamp c1930
Work-worn men enjoying the 'luxurious' seat at the Victoria Lamp during a spell of hot weather. Their combined ages total 555 years: D. Few 83 years, D. Warland 86 years, I. Searle 91 years, G. Taylor 76 years, F. Norman 70 years, H. Porter 74 years and A. Pont 75 years.

34 Lambs Lane

The Gas Works was built in 1862. The first Gas Company house was built in 1864 and the coal to make the gas was carted from Oakington Station.

The first man employed to run the Gas Works in Cottenham, Walter Rhodes, was there for about fifteen years from 1865. Several of the men employed to deputise for him were unreliable because of their drinking habits. When Mr Rhodes left, the Gas Company applied to the Salvation Army for a suitable replacement; the Salvation Army members were of course teetotallers. James Coe was employed in the late 1880s, but he left to become a greengrocer. In 1891, William 'Gassy' Moore took over, staying for thirty-two years.

In 1932 the Chesterton Rural District Council bought what was then called the Cottenham Gas and Water Company, paying £500 for the gas section and £4,500 for the water section. Gas street lighting was installed in 1864 from the Gas House to the church. In the 1930s every second lamp was removed and used to light the Lanes. At first the lamps were not lit for two days before or after a full moon as an economy measure. Initially, they had to be lit and snuffed out individually, but eventually a pilot light and a clockwork mechanism was installed. The grey lamp posts with swan necks are still being used having since been converted to electricity. Of the other utilities, mains water was piped to Cottenham from 1903 and electricity came to the village in the early 1930s.

Victory Way

These houses were built on orchards after the Second World War and were first offered to the returned servicemen housed in the Army's nissen huts at 'Ten Acre' field off Histon Road.

Stevens Close, off Victory Way, was named after the long-serving District Nurse Vere Stevens, who came to Cottenham in February 1938. Nurse Stevens boarded with Frederick and May Maskell throughout her career in the village, until she retired in July 1967. At the time of writing this book Nurse Stevens is living in Wales and has reached the age of ninety-seven.

The Dissenters' Cemetery

The Dissenters' Cemetery in 2002

For many years the dissenting community in Cottenham had wished to obtain a place where they could bury their dead, without being subject to the influence of the priests of the established church. An acre of land was eventually purchased in Lambs Lane from James Graves for £280 and the Cottenham Dissenters' Cemetery opened for interment in June 1845. Funds were provided by public subscription and collections amounted to £505 by June 1847. In the early years payments for plots could be made in instalments. In 1913 a further rood was bought from Mr T.W. Graves, and in more recent years land for a further extension on the west side has been obtained by the Board of Trustees.

The Cottenham County Primary School

The Primary School was built on allotment land and first opened for infants only for the summer term on Thursday 24th April 1969. There were seven classrooms, a hall, kitchen and staff room.

The first headmaster, Mr Dethloff, had to divide his time between the infants at Lambs Lane and the juniors who had remained at Margett Street. When he died suddenly, his place was taken by Joseph Clark, and then by Paul Stone who retired in 2001. The present headteacher is Mrs Jan Wright. Ten years after the school opened seven more classrooms and the cloakrooms had been built, allowing the juniors to be moved to the Lambs Lane site. The old school bell and drinking water fountain were brought from the Margett Street School and placed in the lobby. Gradually the number of children enrolled grew so that four mobile classrooms were required; these remained in place for many years until another suite of rooms was added.

The Recreation Ground

This was created from some existing allotments in 1935 after fund-raising augmented by the King George V Memorial Fund. Once opened, all village recreational activities transferred to this site.

Manse Drive

The red brick house on the corner was once lived in by pastors of the Ebenezer Chapel. Manse Drive was named for this reason.

The Water Tower Conversion

The Lambs Lane windmill being converted for use as a water tower after the Cottenham Gas and Water Company purchased it in 1898

Riveters at work on the conversion in 1903
The sound of the rivets being driven in could be heard throughout the village.

The water supply pipes being laid
Two hundred and sixty-seven houses were supplied with mains water by 1910.

Cottenham Waterworks, drawn by Olwyn Peacock, from 'Cottenham's Troubled Waters' (1978)

Rampton Road

During the First World War servicemen were billeted under canvass on a flying field near North Fen Farm off Rampton Road, with orders to shoot down any of the German Zeppelin airships that flew over the village.

One Rampton Road resident remembers hearing the very first sounding of the air-raid siren at Charles Lack & Sons at the beginning of the Second World War. Many of the residents came out of their houses and were seen by the air-raid warden Mr Hart, who shouted, 'Take cover, Take cover!' as he cycled down the road to the Green. Each street was allocated two tin helmets and a stirrup pump and these had to be passed along to whoever was doing duty as an air-raid warden.

Little London Almshouses, Cottenham

25-39 Rampton Road

The Little London Almshouses were eight cottages built in Tudor style, in 1853, on parish land sold to Moreton's Charity for £60. There was an Anglican chapel in the centre, opened on 7th March 1855, where services were held for the benefit of the inhabitants. The chapel has since been converted into two houses. The houses were modernised in 1961 with money raised by the sale of the Church End Almshouses. This photograph is dated 11th February 1911. On the far right is Amos Norman, in a cart drawn by his horse Daisy.

Ellis Close

The Close, which was named after Dr Ellis, was built upon a grass field that formed part of the Harlestons Manor owned by Christ's College. Dr Ellis' surgery was at The Limes in the High Street, where he practised from 1921 until his retirement after the Second World War.

10-20 Rampton Road

The Labour Exchange, which had occupied this site, closed during the 1960s. If you were unemployed you had to take the next job available, whether or not you wanted that type of work. There was far more seasonal employment than now, and most of the jobs available were of a manual nature. The Labour Exchange served Oakington, Rampton and Willingham as well as Cottenham. The manager was Arthur Norman, who was succeeded by his niece Ethel. Conveniently, they lived in the house next to the Exchange.

Histon Road

It is said that when one of his daughters became twenty-one, the seventh Thomas Ivatt planted twenty-one poplar trees along Histon Road in celebration. Only one of the trees remains today.

13 Histon Road

This house was known as Hobson's House because it was one of three houses in Cottenham owned by Hobson's Charity. Before the charity purchased it in 1632, it had been known as 'Derby's'.

John Hart had a foundry here in Hobson's House after he came from Hertfordshire in 1862. John, and then his son William, sold ploughshares and other small iron goods from a shop at the left of the house. Harry Hart bought the house from the charity in 1948.

68-80 Histon Road - Fulmer Cottages

These houses were built by John Munsey on land awarded to him at the Cottenham Enclosure in 1842. The land, which had been quarried for ballast, was low lying; hence the original name of Foulmire.

During the Second World War a searchlight unit was based at 'Ten Acre', which is down the Between Close Drove - also known as the Driftway - next to 83 Histon Road near to the village boundary. One Cottenham resident, who frequently cycled home in the dark after working late, recalls the searchlights illuminating her way as she left Histon and came down Barrow Hill. She also remembers hearing the sound of machine gunfire from a German plane as it tried to destroy the searchlight.

Cottenham escaped major damage during the war although it was situated between the Oakington and Waterbeach airfields. There was also a dummy airfield at Great North Fen. The bombers taking off and landing at these bases were a frequent sight. They could sometimes be spotted returning damaged, with only two of their four propellers turning. One British plane crash-landed at the cut at Rampton; a local man, Samuel Fletcher, helped to rescue one of the airmen from the wreckage. On another occasion, two spitfires were seen flying very low over the village as they forced a German plane to land at Oakington Airfield.

Incendiary bombs were dropped in Rooks Street, North Fen and just outside of the village on Oakington Road, but fortunately there were no injuries.

A view of Histon Road towards the Dunstal Field site

Dunstal Field

The first football team formed in Cottenham, in 1899 by the Wesley Guild, played on Thomas Ivatt's grass field, which is now part of the Dunstal Field estate.

In the back row are Ernest Sanderson, William Collins, Fred Leader, and Constable Rayner the village policeman. In the next row are Walter Collins, Harry Collins and Harry Pauley. In the front row are Tom Smith, Joe Leete, Mr Gibbons, unknown, and Ernest Cooke.

The Cottenham Show

The Cottenham Show and Sports Event started in July 1885 as a small flower show. It was held annually on the Village College site until it moved to Mr Ivatt's grass field in 1900. In the next few years, there was a Horse and Foal Show in the morning and in the afternoon athletics and cycling events took place; there was also a brass band and donkey races. The 1900 Foal Show attracted 160 entries, but, by 1926, horses no longer featured on the programme. The last show was held in 1931. The housing estate was built in 1965.

Rural Industries

The Windmills of Cottenham

The four windmills in Cottenham did a brisk trade in flour and grist until the late 1880s. After the mills closed, Smiths the machinists installed a milling plant on the High Street with a 17bhp oil fired engine.

This mill on Rampton Road was a smock mill owned by the Goode family; Alfred Ansell hired it from them until it ceased work in 1912. Steam power had been added in 1858.

William Ward built the Histon Road windmill, *c*1850. When its construction was proposed, he was told that there was not enough wind in Cottenham for another mill! Ward's mill was also a smock type, with steam power added. It ceased milling *c*1890 and was demolished in 1895.

The Lambs Lane windmill was built by William Graves in 1842 and later operated by Whitehead Smith and his son Henry. It was the only tower mill in Cottenham and was never powered by steam. It was sold in 1898 at auction for £315 to the Cottenham Gas and Water Company.

This smock mill at Millfield off Rooks Street was originally owned by Robert Norman, who died in 1746, and later by the Ivatt family until 1894. On the left with the miller's cart are John Graves and a boy. Against the mill door are Stephen Fullstone, Arthur Furbank and Fred Easy. On the roadway is Joe Rich, the foreman. In the cart on the right is Jacob Smith. Behind the cart is James Graves, the engine driver.

Basket Making

William Munsey's basket making business, established in 1860 at 231-235 High Street, was one of several firms making a large range of baskets for the fruit-growing industry, as well as furniture. William Munsey died in 1890, after which his two sons Ellis and Josiah took over the business.

Rod peelers stripping bark from osiers for Munsey c1900

In the back row, from the left are Ernest Munsey, Mrs Fred Thoday, unknown, unknown, Mrs Alfred Gifford, and Miss Sanderson.

In the front row are unknown, Mrs William Milton and Mrs Richard Croxon and her daughter.

Drawing by Olwyn Peacock, from 'Cottenham's Orchards and Gardens: Domesday to 1990' (1990)

The Varsity Lounge Chair being made by Jack Chapman

A completed Varsity Chair
The university would send out a man weighing at least eighteen stone to test the strength of the chairs before they would take delivery.

Rural Industries: Basket Making

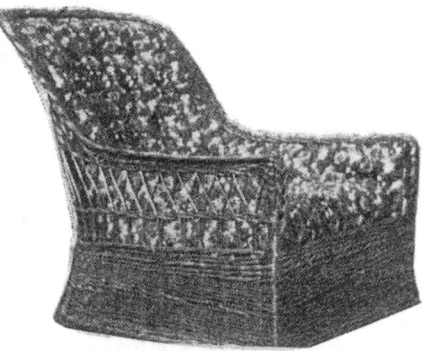

Munsey's advertisement for the Varsity Chair

Charles Moore, another basket maker, operated at the Maltings in Millfield, which is situated off Rooks Street.

The local fruit-growing industry required large numbers of different types of baskets. The willow was grown locally, along osier holts.

Tales are told of how, before the First World War, at Walter Phillips' basket making business in Rooks Street, the children hired to strip the bark from the willow hid in the shavings and dared not to sneeze when the one-legged school inspector known as 'Peg Leg', came around looking for truants.

Pigeon baskets made by Charles Moore

These baskets were traditionally made with two compartments: the cock birds would be kept on one side and the hen birds on the other. From the left are Sidney Bennerson, Charles Moore, Jack Chapman, Stanley Smith and William Golding.

Dairying

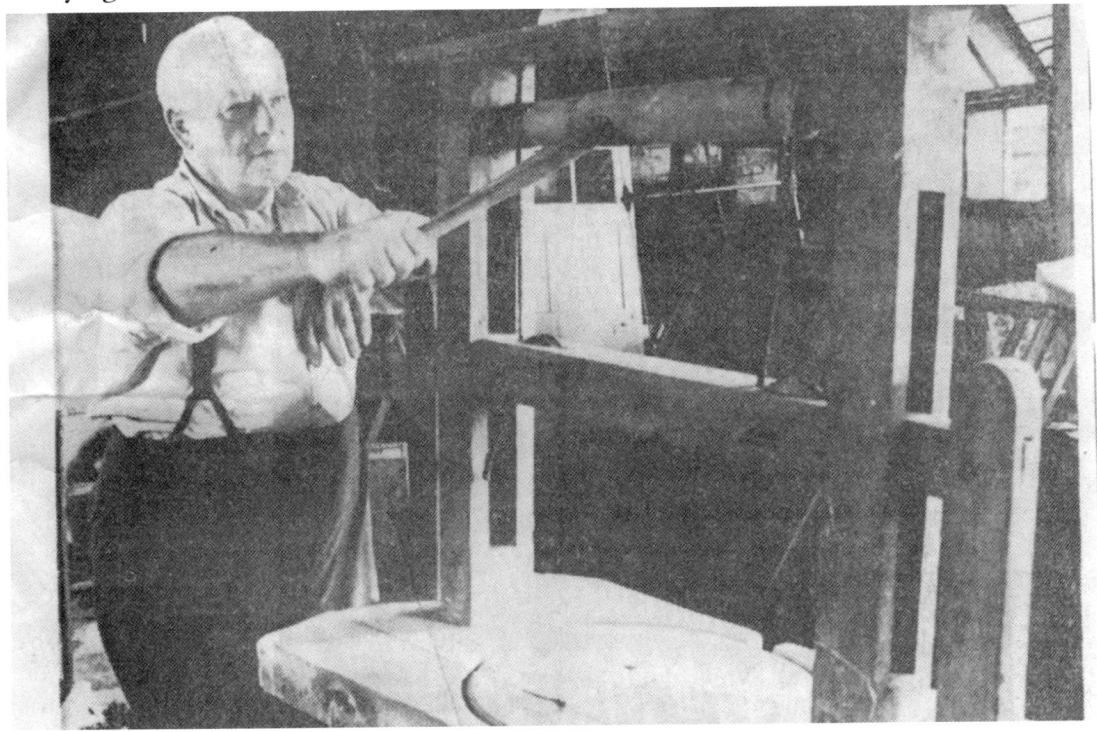

A wooden cheese press

Cecil Gautrey is pictured with the wooden cheese press he removed from the dairy at 337 High Street when Mr Collins died in 1972.

The industry dates back to the thirteenth century when dairy products, including cheese, were supplied to Crowland Abbey from the manor in Cottenham. By the 17th century there was single Cottenham cheese, which was a soft cream cheese, and double Cottenham cheese, the more famous blue cheese.

Double Cottenham cheese, a whitish yellow cheese and blue veined like Stilton, was known all over England before the 1842 Enclosure. According to G.A. Cooke's *Topographical and Statistical Description of the County of Cambridgeshire* dated 1807, 'The superiority of the Cottenham cheese, so famous throughout England, is not to be ascribed to any particular mode in the management of the dairies, but solely to the herbage on the commons'.

Markets such as the internationally famous Stourbridge Fair in Cambridge were supplied, and some was sent to London. Almost every house in the village had its own dairy and cheese room in the 17th and 18th centuries. Before the Enclosure Act of 1842, Cottenham had a population of 1,500 people and 1,200 milking cows. 4,000 acres of pasture land were ploughed up in the land redistribution, leaving little room for grazing so that production of double Cottenham cheese was severely curtailed. The final blow came with the cattle plague of 1865, which killed most of the remaining stock.

A stone cheese press

This stone cheese press is the only remaining example in place in Cottenham. It was last used by the Bull family during the 19th century.

A milk-cooling machine being used at Thomas Graves' farm at Smithy Fen

Cold water was piped from a cold water container to the radiator system, which cooled the warm milk as it passed over the cold surface. From the left are William Norman, Norman Parker, Isaac Everitt, Wright Ambrose and Jack Green.

Horticulture

Soft fruit was grown on a large scale in Cottenham from the 1880s until the 1960s.

At its peak, the soft fruit industry supported ten carriers in Cottenham, who transported the fruit to Oakington Station where it was consigned mainly to northern towns like Manchester and Blackburn, with some also going to London. There was never any guarantee that the fruit would be sold once it got to the market. If it was damaged or there was a glut of fruit, the fruit could not be sold. The fruit-grower would receive no money from the market, but would still have to pay the carriage.

Local people would complain of another consignment going 'Down the Nile', because the returns coming back of unsold fruit would be marked 'Nil' written with a curly 'L', which local growers read as 'Nile'.

Many Cottenham fruit-growers were smallholders, who would have to seek credit from local shopkeepers, or take other employment in the lean months of the winter and early spring.

Chivers first made jam during a glut of fruit in 1873 and established a factory in Histon in 1875. They encouraged the planting of soft fruit and plums, and in 1901, when Rider Haggard visited the area, he noted that in Cottenham there were many small growers with holdings of three to twenty acres. He stated that Chivers offered a 'ready and profitable market for their produce, without carriage to pay, or the intervention of the middle man'. However, growers did have to accept the price offered by Chivers.

Pat Moore, the farmer, fruit-grower and amateur jockey, puffing insecticide powder on raspberry canes in 1936

Mrs Cyril Easy at her strawberry field on Oakington Road showing a 4lb chip of strawberries in the late 1930s

Mr and Mrs Cyril Easy's strawberry field in the late 1930s

Mr and Mrs Cyril Easy with their Clara Butt tulips in the late 1930s

Harry Gautrey with cucumbers in his greenhouse in Beach Road c1905

A trolley loaded with bushel sieves (which contained 40lb of fruit, usually apples) at Arthur Bull's fruit farm in the 1890s. Mr Bull had one of the larger fruit-growing businesses in Cottenham. He produced all the locally grown types of top-fruit: apples, pears and plums.

Arthur Bull (d.1920)

Mr Bull was also a local historian who wrote articles about Cottenham for the Parish Magazine from 1893 to 1901. He was an expert on fen drainage and, aged seventy, he cycled many miles around the fens, gathering information about the Southery, Hockwold and Methwold district floods.

Agriculture

Nearly all Cottenham inhabitants were involved in agriculture until the First World War.

Before the Enclosure of 1842, the highland of the village (1,576 acres) was divided into five Open Fields – Dunstal Field, Church Field, Farm Field, Two Mill Field and Further Field. This land was cropped in rotation with wheat, barley, peas and beans and again barley with roots, turnips and potatoes, leaving one field fallow each year. The majority of plots within the fields were measured in furlongs and were about half an acre each. People had a strip in each of the fields to even out their income.

The lower lying areas were common land and mainly used as pasture, but after the Enclosure, these fenland fields changed to arable farmland.

With the agricultural depression of the 1870s, much of Cottenham's agricultural land was planted with orchards or market gardens. In the 1960s, nearly a century later, the emphasis changed back to agriculture.

Men loading corn in the fen before the First World War
Note the six-foot wide hay rake, which was used to rake in the loose corn. The grain was collected in sheaves and loaded onto a tumbril cart. The whole family would be involved in the harvest.

Eric Wilkin, carting corn for a local farmer in the mid-1930s
The crop was brought back from the fields to stack in farmyards in the village to wait for threshing in the winter months.

A chain-driven threshing engine belonging to Maskell's firm, built in 1879 by the engineering firm Savages of King's Lynn and photographed in William Bull's stackyard in about 1885. Savages was well known for building fairground equipment as well as agricultural machinery. There were two firms of threshing engineers in Cottenham, the Maskells and the Smiths. The Maskell family business was located at 50 High Street until it ceased threshing in 1928.

A portable steam engine owned by George Chapman when he lived in this cottage at Church Hill (now 3 High Street)

A combine harvester shortly after the Second World War
John Moore is standing at the front, his son Michael is in the driver's seat and Benjamin Moore is in the background.

The Cottenham Feast

The Cottenham Feast is held annually on the first Sunday after 11th October. A highlight of the village calendar was the parade, which was first organised on 14th October 1894 by the Friendly Societies, to raise money for the old Addenbrookes Hospital in Cambridge. The village was crowded with visitors and the public houses were especially full. The children of the village eagerly awaited the festivities. Vehicles bringing the feast attractions were parked in the streets surrounding the Green until they were allowed on to their allotted space at 5 p.m., after the Sunday Parade.

The Feast Week continued until Wednesday. Feast Tuesday was the day when the Fancy Dress Parade was held and the school and shops would close for half a day. Members of the Metropolitan Police Force would come to the village to play football against Cottenham and were entertained to tea at the Social Retreat public house at 319 High Street.

One Cottenham resident recalls that even in the 1950s, when there was no Sunday Parade, many children would wear their new winter coats and shoes for the first time on Feast Sunday.

The Friendly Societies

The ladies shown representing the Friendly Societies are Miss Violet Wilkin, Mrs Gander, Mrs Herbert Bishop, Miss Florrie Sutton, and Miss Emma Bennett.

To quote from the 1921 calendar of the Independent Order of Oddfellows: 'Friendly Societies are beneficial and educational orders for men, women and children, with branches spread throughout the English speaking world, for the insurance of benefits during periods of sickness, in old age and at death'.

The Sunday Feast Parade

In the 1920s the Cottenham Sunday Feast Parade started on the High Street outside the White Horse public house and continued along Telegraph Street, Denmark Road and Rooks Street. The parade then turned into the High Street and proceeded to the church, before marching all the way back to the Green, where they dispersed.

The Fancy Dress Parade, 1926

In the back row, from left are D. Gautrey, R. Gautrey, Katherine Waldock, Raymond Stapleton, Winifred Blunt and E. Norman.

In the front row are Grace Pratt, C. Smith, D. Love, Cecily Blunt and Irene Haird.

During the Second World War and up to 1968, there was no parade but the Salvation Army held a service on the Green on Feast Sunday. The Feast Parade was revived in October 1968 by Harry Littlechild and others at the Sports and Social Club when there were six decorated floats headed by the Salvation Army Band. The collection for charity amounted to £58. Nowadays, community groups decorate floats for a parade that travels down the High Street for a service held on the Green, after which the parade returns along Lambs Lane. The participants collect money in all manner of containers, from firemen's helmets to butterfly nets, for the chosen charity.

Church End had its own feast on Shrove Tuesday. Originally stalls were placed in the churchyard, but after about 1800 there were a few stalls outside the churchyard wall, and others going down the High Street to the Jolly Millers yard; these stalls sold small toys, rock and brandy snaps. After the First World War and the beginning of the bus service, the number of stalls decreased, but there are still happy memories of an orange seller and a coconut shy. The Shrove Tuesday Feast ended in the 1930s.

Ploughing Matches

Ploughing matches started in the fields around Cottenham in 1843, a year after the Enclosure, and twenty-three teams competed for eight prizes. In 1920 there were seventy-eight teams of horses and ten tractors. Until 1925, the farmers and the subscribers to the Ploughing Society had their dinner at one public house, usually the Jolly Millers, while the ploughmen had their entertainment at another, usually the Three Horseshoes. In later years, the combined group held their dinner in the Margett Street School Hall. Apart from wartime, ploughing matches have continued ever since and the annual dinner and dance is now held at the Village College.

James Graves, an employee of Bicheno Brothers, won the first prize for a single-furrow ploughing match on 4th December 1907

Robert Norman on his tractor at a ploughing match in 1978

Richard Creek, with his Suffolk Punch horses, at a ploughing match in 1979

Eric Cornell returning home from a ploughing match

Cottenham Racecourse

Early Cottenham horseracing was mainly informal, staged on farmland for wagers between local farmers and wealthy young men at Cambridge University. The Prince of Wales visited in 1870, travelling down Chequers Lane, which was renamed Denmark Road in honour of his wife, Princess Alexandra. Racing became more organised just before the First World War when a prominent Cambridge veterinary surgeon, Mr James G. Runciman, acquired the course from the local farmers, and together with Mr D.G. Marshall, embarked on a series of improvements to the course; the grandstand was erected in 1923. The present site reopened in November 1924 with a steeplechase and hurdle-racing meeting following National Hunt rules. Local farmers whose land was used by the Hunt were given free entry tickets and a sumptuous lunch.

T. J. Wakefield's horse, Double Decker, leading the field at a Cottenham Point-to-Point race meeting in 1948

Cottenham jockey Pat Moore on Tom Wakefield's horse, Victory Arch, after winning the members' race in 1949. He was led in by Dorothy Gawthroup and Alec Burgess.

Pat Moore taking a jump in 1950

The Broad Lane Playing Field

The playing field on Broad Lane was allocated at the 1842 Enclosure.

Skating on Broad Lane in 1905

Skating had long been a popular activity in the village when weather permitted. The playing field was deliberately flooded for this purpose in January 1861, when the water in the cut was at the highest level ever known.

When a sharp frost was predicted, water would be pumped from the cut until it flooded the ground to a depth of about four inches. Either John Hart or the Norman brothers would carry out the work for the Parish Council.

The Cottenham Cricket Team, 1924, with the trophies they won in the Milton and District competitions

In the back row, from the left are Gilbert Dorr, Fred Pont, Alva Burgess, Harry Ivatt, Ted Rogers, Ben Moore, and Claude Jacklin.

In the front row are William Thulbourn (scorer), Ted Badcock, Dr Robert Ellis, Nash Rogers (captain), James Moore, S. Camps, and Henry Bowers (umpire).

Amateur Dramatics

Cottenham Dramatic Society
The Cottenham Dramatic Society performed the comedy *Nothing But The Truth* in January 1929 at the Margett Street School. From the left are Bert Greenall, Elsie Gautrey, May Camps, Harold Gautrey, Grace Smith, Kate Chapman, W.W. Greenall, Winifred Gautrey, Eddie Potter, Frank Greenall, Joyce Munsey and popping his head around the screen, Leslie Greenall.

A skit from 'Revueing the Situation', June 1977
Standing, from the left are John Unwin, Reginald Young, David King (obscured), Vera Hughes, Glenda Snooks, unknown, Roger Daw, unknown (obscured), Jill Powell, Margaret Harrison, unknown, Queenie Blunt, unknown, Rosemary Gawood, Julia Daft, Jasper Kay, John Buttifant, Beatrice Tomlinson and Dennis Badcock.
  Seated, are Jane Harrison (obscured), Jeanette Hurworth, Sasha Badcock, Philippa Levy, Sarah Stinton and Sarah Harrison.

The programme cover for the Silver Jubilee revue

The Cottenham Theatre Workshop was formed in 1977 to perform *Revueing the Situation*, a one-off production, as part of the village celebrations for the Silver Jubilee. The group enjoyed themselves so much that they produced a pantomime the following Christmas, entitled *The Witch and the Monster (and a lot of nice people as well)*.

Twenty-five years later they continue to entertain Cottenham with productions of a very high standard; the cast and crew, some of whom are original members, are drawn mainly from the village.

The Cottenham Village Society

The Society was formed in late 1970, its aims being:

— to stimulate public interest in and care for the beauty, history and character of the village and its surroundings

— to encourage the preservation, development and improvement of features of general public amenity or historic interest

— to encourage high standards of architecture and village planning in the Parish of Cottenham and also by supporting other village groups

— to pursue those ends by means of meetings, exhibitions, lectures and promotion of schemes of a charitable nature.

Membership is open to all who are interested in the aims of the Society.